A Parent's Playbook for Learning

Jen Lilienstein

THERE ARE 8 TYPES OF LEARNERS

FIND OUT WHICH ONES YOUR KIDS ARE
AND COACH THEM TO GREATER
SCHOOL SUCCESS.

1

Published by Frontsiders, LLC
PO Box 1478, Summerland, CA 93067—www.kidzmet.com

ISBN 978-0-9884757-9-3

Printed in the United States of America.
First Edition

Table of Contents

Introduction

When my daughter was born, it became clear to me very quickly how different her spirit was from both mine and her Dad's. She not only enjoyed different activities, she innately approached problem-solving, communication, and new environments differently.

Once I got her into enrichment activities, the differences became even clearer. In many cases, the teachers I adored she didn't click with...and the teachers I didn't connect with easily, she couldn't wait to see again. These early learning relationships shaped her perceptions of the subjects.

In fact, the subjects didn't seem to matter as much as the relationship she had with the teacher.

I had similar experiences when I was young. When

I felt a teacher got me, I pushed myself harder to earn high marks, willingly tried things I may not have tried otherwise, and (most importantly) couldn't wait to get back to class and see what new things I would learn about next.

We understand the importance of personality type compatibilities with respect to choosing a spouse. (eHarmony anyone?) Many of us have ventured to a High School Career Center to complete a profile questionnaire that will help us establish the lines of work we're best suited for. Major corporations throughout the world use personality type to help with team building, improving corporate communication and in leadership training. And who among us doesn't have a friend or two who has experienced a quarter- or mid-life crisis because they have spent their lives to that point trying to be someone they just *weren't*.

The thing is, honoring our personality type and innate strengths isn't just important to us as adults. Learning how to get organized, tackle challenges, plan ahead, communicate effectively, and solve problems in ways that play to our strengths—all these can reap huge rewards, from the classroom to the boardroom and everywhere in between.

Just because certain learning, study or organizational techniques worked well for you as a child (or work well for you now) doesn't mean they will work equally as well for all your children. We've developed this "Playbook for Learning" as an easy-to-use guide for parents that goes beyond learning Google-able information. Instead, we reveal specific, research-backed, proven techniques and actionable strategies amassed from nearly 100 reference texts that help your child learn in the most effective, efficient ways for his unique spirit.

Four things to keep in mind as you read this book:

1. It has been designed for the average learner.

2. If you suspect or your child has been diagnosed with a learning difference or behavior disorder, we recommend that you use these tactics in addition to those recommended by an expert in how to treat your child's specific learning challenges.

3. This book will be most effective when shared with and put into practice by all of your child's caregivers—spouse, grandparent, nanny, tutor, etc. I cannot emphasize enough how important it is for your child to have all of you on the same page.

4. Don't try to change everything at once. Put a maximum of two or three recommendations into practice at a time, then stick to them. These small, daily habit changes slowly stack on top of each other until eventually your child will develop a treasure trove of effective study habits that he can pull from.

We hope it helps make education and learning more effective, efficient and **fun** for BOTH of you!

Jen Lilienstein, Founder, Kidzmet.com

Your Child's Unique Personality Profile

"Different kids learn differently."

~Kurt W. Fischer,

Director of Harvard University's

Mind, Brain, and Education Program

Your Child's Unique Personality Profile

You'll often hear people remark about how a child got his father's ears or his grandmother's nose. Similarly, your child's temperament is a blend of his parents' and grandparents' personality type preferences. The following pages present the key pieces of your child's "personality puzzle," and perhaps reveal a clearer picture of how those traits blend to form his complete personality profile.

Be sure to spend a few moments reviewing the comparisons on the next four pages to make sure you reference the content in this book that is right for your child. These descriptions will also give you a clearer sense of who in your family to lean on or talk to during more challenging times, and how to tackle any issues from someone who has lived and breathed it.

Extravert or Introvert?

Which of the following sounds MORE like your child?

Extraverted	Introverted
Like to be the ones TALKING (vs. listening)	Energized with alone time or time with 1 or 2 friends
Enjoy having LOTS of friends around (vs. one or two)	Will THINK about a question BEFORE volunteering an answer—especially if the idea is new
Feel comfortable around people they've never met	
	May hesitate to speak up unless invited
Process initial thoughts better by talking them out (thinking aloud)	Quiet and reserved around NEW people, but may talk your ear off if they know you well!
Enjoy being the center of attention	

Remember this preference, then move on to the next page.

Judger or Perceiver?

Which of the following sounds MORE like your child?

JUDGER	PERCEIVER
Organized and purposeful, judgers focus on the DESTINATION	Open, curious and interested, perceivers choose to focus on the JOURNEY
Like to FOLLOW the rules	Find rules confining and will often bend rules if they don't make sense to them
Approach assignments like an ENDURANCE RUNNER - with the self-control to work at a certain pace to get done by a specified deadline	Approach assignments like a SPRINTER and thrive on the energy of a looming deadline
SYSTEMATIC - prefer to stick to a game plan	Thrive under PRESSURE
Don't like to change their minds after they've reached a conclusion	SPONTANEOUS and ADAPTABLE, they like to keep their options open

IF YOU RESPONDED EXTRAVERT+JUDGER OR INTROVERT+PERCEIVER, SKIP THE NEXT PAGE.

Sensor or Intuitive?

Which of the following sounds MORE like your child?

Sensor	Intuitive
Forms perceptions based on what IS	Forms perceptions based on what COULD BE
Remembers details, facts and tangible specifics	Likes to focus on the main idea, and may miss details
Most engaged while practicing skills already learned	Most excited about new and different tasks and ideas
Prefer instructions broken into small, sequential, actionable tasks	Prefer general guidelines to specific directions
Enjoys reproducing things that already exist more than designing new things	Looks for patterns, themes, and meaning beneath the surface of things

Skip the next page to reveal the result.

THINKER OR FEELER?

Which of the following sounds MORE like your child?

FEELER	THINKER
Often makes decisions based on WHO will be impacted and HOW	Prefers cause-and-effect decisions based on logic and reason
Prone to interpreting NO feedback as NEGATIVE feedback	Stimulated by problems to be solved and things to fix
Enjoys helping, cooperating with, and pleasing others	Values impartial consistency in application of rules in all cases to all people
Thinks and judges in shades of gray	Thinks and judges in black and white
Values consensus above competition	Values competition above consensus

GO TO THE NEXT PAGE TO REVEAL THE RESULT.

Personality Types

Below are the personality types and associated icons you'll find throughout this book. You can choose to read the whole thing or just look for the pages that are appropriate for your children. **Want a more detailed analysis? Take the free preference profile on www. kidzmet.com.**

 EXTRAVERTED FEELER (JUDGER)

 EXTRAVERTED INTUITIVE (PERCEIVER)

 EXTRAVERTED SENSOR (PERCEIVER)

 EXTRAVERTED THINKER (JUDGER)

 INTROVERTED FEELER (PERCEIVER)

 INTROVERTED INTUITIVE (JUDGER)

 INTROVERTED SENSOR (JUDGER)

 INTROVERTED THINKER (PERCEIVER)

Getting Organized ::
Space & Time Management

"If there is anything that we wish to change in the child, we should first examine it and see whether it is not something that could better be changed in ourselves."

~Carl Jung

A hare was once boasting of his speed to the other animals. "I haven't been beaten yet when I go at full speed," he said. "Does anyone want to race?"

The tortoise stepped forward to accept the challenge.

The hare burst out laughing. "What a good joke! I could run circles around you the whole way!"

"Let's just see about that," the tortoise responded. "Shall we race?"

So the animals decided on a course and the hare and tortoise began the race. The hare darted almost out of sight at once, but soon stopped and lay down to have a nap, because he was energized by deadlines and racing wasn't so much fun without the risk of being beaten. The tortoise plodded on and plodded on, knowing that step-by-step was how he would cross the finish line.

Unfortunately, when the hare awoke from his nap,

he saw the tortoise nearing the finish line, and

he could not catch up in time to win the race.

But what would have happened if the

hare had woken up a hair earlier?

And would the tortoise have challenged the

hare in the first place if he didn't know how

to pace himself across the finish line?

In this classic time management fable, the tortoise has a judging personality type and the hare has a perceiving personality type. One is not better than the other...each animal needs to *both* play to his strengths *and* acknowledge his weaknesses.

POP QUIZ!

WHICH OF THE FOLLOWING SPACES IS BETTER ORGANIZED FOR LEARNING SUCCESS?

ROOM 1: Only a single pen and paper on the writing surface (or laptop), a single reference

book, remaining homework tucked away in a
file drawer or backpack, a day timer, no clutter
in the room. A trash can under the desk.

ROOM 2: A jar of pencils, highlighters, dry-erase
markers on the desk, visible bookshelf, dry-erase
board, large calendar that shows the month ahead,
homework in visible file folders, and a squishy
stress ball. A trash can "hoop" across the room
in which to shoot crumpled previous drafts.

ANSWER: IT DEPENDS ON YOUR CHILD'S PERSONALITY TYPE!

This can be one of the hardest things for a parent
to accept...particularly if your child naturally
organizes and plans differently than you!

Getting Organized for Judgers:: Space & Time Management

A PLACE FOR EVERYTHING AND EVERYTHING IN ITS PLACE

The most important thing for a judging child is to keep

their workspace clear of clutter and have a set place

to do homework that is free from sibling interference.

This does not mean that your child needs his or her own

desk or even a space that is dedicated solely to studying.

But, during the time spent doing homework, having a

designated place for "work" will help tremendously.

If your child is lucky enough to have a desk with drawers

in it, two kinds of drawer organizers can be helpful:

1. One with smaller compartments to keep pens, pencils, highlighters, etc., separate

2. A hanging file-folder rack with a folder for each subject and a set of file folders that can

be slipped inside for long-term projects.

If your child doesn't have a desk or his desk does not have drawers purchase a legal-sized accordion file for the year and label each pocket by subject, keeping pockets empty for:

- individual cases for pens/pencils, highlighters, crayons/colored pencils, etc.

- additional loose-leaf paper

- file folders for long-term projects

Not sure what school supplies your child will need for this year in school? This list from GreatSchools.org can help: http://bit.ly/KkBos8

It's incredibly important for a judging child like your child to have an "out" box. Judgers delight in the destination and in bringing things to closure, so placing homework in the "out" box as it's completed can be incredibly satisfying for your child.

TIME MANAGEMENT

In this same vein, keeping a to-do list in a day timer

can also help your child feel good about everything

that's been accomplished during the day.

Help your child prioritize daily homework

and chores by what can get done fast FIRST,

so that the still-to-do list shrinks quickly.

One technique that works well is to print daily chore

lists out on Avery 5163 labels that your child can peel

off and stick in the day-timer in the morning (or at the

beginning of the week), then add homework to the to-do

list during the day. Again, be sure to put the chores that

can be completed quickly at the beginning of the list.

SLOW AND STEADY WINS THE RACE

When a long-term project is assigned, grab a file

folder and tape a project timeline (from page 92 or on

Kidzmet's printable template CD) to the outside of the folder, then decide with your child what interim steps need to be accomplished to finish the project and how much time your child will need for each interim step.

Help your child break the time allotted for the assignment up into daily work on the project and add each task to his day-timer.

Encourage your child to cross items off the ladder to show how much closer your child is getting to achieving the goal.

Praise your child for bringing each project phase to closure...especially if it's ahead of time!

When Things Don't Go As Planned

If a section of a project is taking longer than anticipated, be patient as you help your child develop a back-up plan. The anxiety these kids experience when an original plan isn't working can feel strange for a perceiving parent who naturally is flexible/spontaneous and is energized by a deadline. While timing is a natural gift of judgers like your child, coping when things don't go as planned is more of a challenge.

If your child is involved in a group project, getting the kids together after school so that there is agreement on what will be finished when can ease your child's fears of not having enough time to get things done.

Comfort in Routine

Unlike perceivers, judging kids like your child thrive with daily routine. For this reason, it's a good idea to include your child in decisions about

extracurricular activities or family holidays, as they

may have input related to upcoming school work or

which days of the week have more homework that

you'll want to include in your planning process.

Getting your child involved in family plans and

decisions also honors and celebrates your child's

natural gift for timing, planning, and decision-making.

Space & Time Management for Perceivers

SET THE STAGE

For a judging parent who needs a clear workspace before starting work on a new project, a cluttered desk—even if it's organized—can seem like starting off on the wrong foot. Not so for your perceiving child, however.

Because out of sight truly *is* out of mind for perceivers, and your child is energized by deadlines, it's best to have an organized file folder inbox on the desk so that your child can see how much work lies ahead or is due. Allow him to create a filing system that feels right. While you may feel better with a filing system that is categorized by subject, your child may feel better with a due-date system or a long-to-short activity system. Allowing for this creative approach to filing not only

honors your child's nature, but also helps ensure that files are put together in ways that make sense to him. (You probably know a few grown-up perceivers who know exactly where to find paperwork when they need it...even if no one else can figure out their filing system.)

Nightly to-dos should be placed in the appropriate boxes the moment that your child arrives home from school. Once work is complete, it should go right into his backpack. (As you've probably already noticed, keeping track of items can be a real challenge for perceivers like your child.)

If your child is lucky enough to have a desk, two kinds of organizers can be helpful:

- A desktop organizer that keeps everything in view, from scissors and staplers to glue and tape, to pens and highlighters. (Be sure to get a stack of post-its for your little perceiver.)

- A stacked file-folder rack with a folder for each subject and a set of file folders that can be slipped inside for long-term projects.

If your child doesn't have a desk, a scrapbook organizer can serve as a satellite study station for the year. Fill pockets with:

- individual cases for pens/pencils, highlighters, crayons/colored pencils, etc.

- additional loose-leaf paper

- file folders for long-term projects and nightly to-dos

Regardless of whether your child has a desk or not, we highly recommend purchasing a dry-erase white board with several different colored dry-erase markers for your child's room to be used for long-term project brainstorming. (More on this later.)

TIME MANAGEMENT

As a perceiver, your child likes to live in the

realm of possibilities and will often "noodle"
on things before getting down to business.

Perceiving kids like your child also like to blend work
and play. Judging parents may find themselves tearing
their hair out and pleading with their little Perceiver
to *focus* or *just get it done* while he makes jokes,
tosses a stress ball in the air, or takes brain breaks
for a quick game of Angry Birds. The reality is that
perceivers are energized by deadlines and naturally
don't like to finalize things until absolutely necessary.

This said, while perceivers have a gift for adaptability
and spontaneity, they need to be coached into better
time management. Unlike judgers, perceivers work
better with an at-a-glance calendar, on which they
can mark important due dates, upcoming events, etc.
Being able to see one or two months at a time can be
extremely helpful in ensuring that your child doesn't

have too many balls in the air to catch at the same time.

ONE DAY AT A TIME

One way to do this with nightly homework is to help
him prioritize homework by what will take *longest*
first, and what can be done *quickly* last. Then, work on
interim deadlines like, "Your math homework must
be done before dinner or there's no X tonight," or
"Your language arts homework must be done before
you watch any TV tonight." Breaking tasks up in this
way will help ensure that there's time for everything,
and that your child will have an opportunity to break
up work with short bursts of play at minimum.

IN IT FOR THE LONG HAUL

When a long-term project is assigned, print out a
copy of a project tree from page 91 or from Kidzmet's
printable template CD. Better yet, draw the trunk and
branches on your child's whiteboard, then, working
backward from the final deadline, decide how much

time your child will need to complete each interim step (these will differ by project type). Don't forget to leave space for a materials list on the board. Finally, encourage your child to add post-it note "leaves" to the project tree when inspiration strikes.

Your child's perceiving/last-minute nature can pose a challenge with group projects...particularly if he is paired up with judging teammates. For this reason, it's good to look at due dates and break them up into two interim dates: the first at the halfway mark for brainstorming, the second the day before the assignment is due to the other team member. In this way, you can make sure that some thought is given to assignments well in advance of the due date and your child will end up with a more thoughtful contribution as a result. However, you're still honoring your child's innate need to keep his options open by not asking for the final deliverable until it's truly due.

Approaching New Concepts

"The younger the learner, the less likely they are able to adapt to the task when the task does not match their style. Understanding type concepts helps...students stretch to learn new skills while using their strengths to master difficult concepts"

~MMTIC The Chemistry of Personality:

Guide to Interaction in the Classroom

Meisgeier, C. H., & Murphy, E. (1987)

*O*nce upon a time, four blind men came upon an elephant. "What is this?" asked the first one, who had run head-first into its side.

"It's an elephant," said the elephant's keeper.

The first man, running his hands as far as he could reach up and down the elephant's side, exclaimed, "Why, it's just like a wall, a large, warm wall!"

The second man, with his arms around the elephant's leg, disagreed: "This is nothing like a wall. You can't reach around a wall! This is more like a pillar. Yeah, that's it, an elephant is exactly like a pillar!"

"You're both wrong," said the third man, stroking the elephant's trunk. "If you think this is a pillar, I don't want to go to your house! This elephant is thin, flexible and even wrapping itself around my arm. It's just like a snake!"

"You're all crazy!" the fourth man cried, waving the elephant's ear back and forth. "It's like a large piece of

cloth, thin as a leaf. No one in their right mind could

mistake an elephant for anything except a sail!"

And as the elephant moved on, they stumbled along

down the road, arguing more vehemently as they

went, each sure that he alone was right and all

the others' perceptions were wrong. Whereas the

reality is that an elephant is... an elephant.

In education, each new concept is an elephant
to students. And different personality types will
understand different aspects of the elephant first.
We need to make sure, as parents, that we honor
these preferred "entry points," so that our kids
come at concept-understanding in ways that play
to their innate learning strengths...even if their
natural entry point is different than our own.

Approaching New Concepts with an EFJ Child

You've probably noticed that your child has a unique gift for seeing the best in people. This compassion and concern relates not just to living beings, but also to deeply-held values, beliefs and ideals—even if not always openly expressed or in alignment with cultural norms.

Because extraverted feelers like your child want most to maintain harmony, he will make choices about learning new concepts that keep the peace with his study groups, peers, teachers and parents... even if it means creating a bit of an internal conflict for himself. The good news is, this typically means that your child will do his best for both you and his teachers...particularly if a caring and warm personal relationship has been established. What he needs most—especially when approaching new concepts—is help understanding how the new concept supports the values of his world, culture, and community.

CONVERSATIONAL CHAMELEON

Your child's learning strength and weakness lie in his ability to adapt his behavior and conversational style to any group. Extraverted feelers like your child have an almost uncanny instinct for quickly detecting cultural norms and niceties, then applying them.

In order to get your child really excited about a subject, talk with him about it before sending him into the "solo zone" to work through homework. Be aware that he needs this discussion with you to talk out his understanding of how to apply the concept. If he's not "getting it," try relating stories with similar patterns that illustrate the human, social or emotional impact of the concept.

The most important part is to provide the opportunity

for the dialogue that allows your child to both construct and reconstruct his understanding of the material and help him build the consensus that is so important to extraverted feelers.

This discuss → reflect/attempt → discuss learning progression resonates strongly for parents who are also extraverts, but for introverted parents can seem just... well...wrong. Introverts by nature prefer to reflect on new information first before discussing it. Introverts also won't typically voice a thought or opinion unless they're sure it's correct. Extraverts, on the other hand, *talk* their way to understanding, so in most cases what they say is not necessarily a complete or final thought.

Even the ways in which conversation is structured is different for introverts. Extraverts will interrupt and talk over other voices during the discussion phase, but will need quiet to focus and concentrate during the reflection phase.

CAN'T WE ALL JUST GET ALONG?

Because your child's understandings need to take

into account the needs, desires and values of those

around him, introducing new concepts that have

individuals staunchly on either side of the debate—

for instance, abortion, immigration, politics—can

be very uncomfortable for your child. In some cases,

your child may flip-flop his position based on the

perspective of the group. Because of his innate pull to

build consensus, it can be extremely challenging for

your child to simply "agree to disagree." This can even

be seen to the extent that he substitutes "I" for "we"

when talking about ideas or answering questions.

If a class or teacher thrives on debate or harsh

criticism, your child will most likely have a challenging

time in the class. Extraverted feelers like your child

not only have a hard time hearing the critique

when a teacher is displeased with his answer,
but also tend to personalize the embarrassment
or discomfort of other students in the class.

Your Child is a Linear Learner

It's important to help your child develop a step-
by-step approach to concept understanding.

One technique that can work particularly well is to teach
him to skim a paragraph or passage once, then go back
and highlight, underline or make note of the key parts
of the paragraph. Repeat this process until the required
reading is complete, then assemble the detail building
blocks he has identified into a more general idea.

If your child is struggling, help him to identify the key
details required for understanding, or show him a
formula, process or procedure to follow. Map out an
approach to take, then identify priorities and create a
structure he can follow to achieve the desired outcome.

WORD CHOICE MATTERS

It's incredibly important to key into language that will

open your child up (versus close him down). Here's

a start to the list of words to use and avoid with your

child...at least until his interest in the subject matter is

piqued.

USE	AVOID
Express	Critique
Cooperate	Debate
Contribute	Generate
Assist	Synthesize
Suggest	Examine
Share	Compute
Help	Systematize
Clarify	Categorize
Request	Fix
Translate	Assemble
Survey	Order
Reflect	Determine
Feel	Assess

Approaching New Concepts with an ENP Child

You've probably noticed that your child dives headlong into new interests and friendships and can't wait to try new things.

This pull toward the novel and your child's innate "bring it on!" attitude can make approaching *new* concepts much easier on you when helping with homework. There's actually some brain chemistry at work that causes this.

THAT'S DOPE!

Neuroscientists have recently discovered that dopamine is the brain chemical at work that causes us to seek out, search and want. For your child, he craves interaction and discussion in order to seek out new information or search for new perspectives. In order to get your child really excited about a subject, talk to him about it before sending him into the "solo zone" to finish homework. Or, if you're not available for this conversation, recruit your spouse or a close relative, or plan study groups with other extraverts in your child's class.

The most important part is to allow for the dialogue that allows your child to both construct and reconstruct his understanding of the material.

This discuss → reflect/attempt → discuss learning progression resonates strongly for parents who are also extraverts, but for introverted parents can seem just... well...wrong. Introverts by nature prefer to reflect on new information first before discussing it. Introverts also won't typically voice a thought or opinion unless they're sure it's correct. Extraverts, on the other hand, talk their way to understanding, so in most cases what they say is not necessarily a complete or final thought.

Even the ways in which conversation is structured

is different for introverts. Extraverts will

interrupt and talk over other voices during the

discussion phase, but will need quiet to focus

and concentrate during the reflection phase.

Don't Sweat the Small Stuff...At Least in the Beginning

Your child's learning strength lies in grasping general

concepts and meanings versus all of the facts and details.

Your child first wants to answer the question, "Why

do I need to learn this?" before diving in. In the grand

scheme of things, your child prefers to be more of a

forest ranger than a tree trimmer. Be sure to use broad

strokes to paint the big picture of the subject in the

beginning, then fill in the details later, because you may

lose your child if you focus on the small stuff too early.

This being said, your child will most likely need your

help during the completion phase of projects to notice

any important details he may have overlooked or to draw
out enough supporting evidence for his conclusions.

A LEARNING DANCE VS. DASH

It's important to allow your child to meander
through material instead of demanding that
he follow a step-by-step approach.

One technique that can work particularly well is to
teach your child to read the chapter wrap-up, then
skim the first sentence of each paragraph, and finally
dig into each aspect of the concept or chapter, starting
with whatever aspect piques his interest most.

In this way, your child will first dance around the topic,
then fill in the puzzle pieces in the way that either
intrigues him or makes most sense to him. And, as
I'm sure you've noticed in other aspects of your child's
life, extraverted intuitives are more enthusiastic about
tasks when they can approach them creatively.

Introducing Mind Maps and Venn Diagrams (both on Kidzmet's printable template CD and in the upcoming chapter on note-taking) are two modeling methods that work well for extraverted intuitives like your child.

In this same vein, allow your child to switch between homework subjects if desired, because his completion pace will slow tremendously if the work becomes too monotonous.

Switching subjects doesn't mean that your child will stop thinking about the new topic. More likely, this brain break will help connect the new knowledge into other areas...particularly if you use the time to discuss and discover other aspects of life in which this new knowledge applies.

Word Choice Matters

It's incredibly important to key into language that will open your child up (versus close him down). Here's a start to the list of words to use and avoid with your child...at least until his interest in the subject matter is piqued. We encourage you to add more words on either side of the fence.

Use	Avoid
Elaborate	Define
Discover	Investigate
Create	Assemble
Dream	Build
Imagine	List
Brainstorm	Examine
Explore	Practice
Synthesize	Review
Develop	Observe
Experiment	Detail
Illustrate	Simplify
Analyze	Discuss

Approaching New Concepts with an ESP Child

You've probably noticed that your child lives in the moment and relishes his role as the life of the party.

Because your child values sensorial enjoyment of all kinds, typically doesn't like rules or restrictions, and has a pull toward multi-tasking, homework can be a real challenge for parents—particularly when introducing new concepts. Luckily, when you approach new concepts in a way that embraces your child's nature, the dopamine rush he experiences will keep him coming back for more learning.

THAT'S DOPE!

Neuroscientists have recently discovered that dopamine is the brain chemical at work that causes us to seek out, search and want. For your child, he craves interaction and discussion in order to seek out new information or search for new perspectives. In order to get your child really excited about a subject, talk to him about it before sending him into the "solo zone" to finish homework. Or, if you're not available for this conversation, recruit your spouse or a close relative, or plan study groups with other extraverts in your child's class.

The most important part is to allow for the dialogue that allows your child to both construct and reconstruct his understanding of the material.

This discuss → reflect/attempt → discuss learning progression resonates strongly for parents who are also extraverts, but for introverted parents can seem just... well...wrong. Introverts by nature prefer to reflect on new information first before discussing it. Introverts also won't typically voice a thought or opinion unless they're sure it's correct. Extraverts, on the other hand, talk their way to understanding, so in most cases what they say is not necessarily a complete or final thought.

Even the ways in which conversation is structured is different for introverts. Extraverts will interrupt and talk over other voices during the discussion phase, but will need quiet to focus and concentrate during the reflection phase.

JUST THE FACTS, MA'AM...AT LEAST IN THE BEGINNING

Your child's learning strength lies in grasping facts and details versus more general concepts. Your child first wants to answer the question "What specifically do I need to learn?" or "How precisely will this assignment be graded?" before diving in. In the grand scheme of things, your child prefers to be more of a tree trimmer than a forest ranger. So be sure to avoid using abstract concepts to "paint the big picture" of the subject in the beginning, but instead start with the facts—

ideally information he takes in with his five senses.

Your child will most likely need your help during the initial phase of projects to establish precisely what is expected of him by the instructor and work through an attack plan.

A Learning Dance vs. Dash

It's important to allow your child to meander through material instead of demanding that he follow a step-by-step approach.

One technique that can work particularly well is to teach your child to read the chapter wrap-up, then skim the first sentence of each paragraph, and finally dig into each aspect of the concept or chapter, starting with whatever aspect piques his interest most.

In this way, your child will first dance around the topic, then fill in the puzzle pieces in the way that either intrigues him or makes most sense to him. And, as I'm sure you've noticed in other aspects of your child's life, extraverted sensors are more enthusiastic about tasks when they can approach them creatively.

For your child, whatever you can do to make new concepts tangible, concrete or sensorial will reap huge dividends.

In this same vein, allow your child to switch between homework subjects if desired, because his completion pace will slow tremendously if the work becomes too monotonous.

Switching subjects doesn't mean that your child will stop thinking about the new topic. More likely, this brain break will help connect the new knowledge into other areas if you use the time to discuss and discover other aspects of life in which this new knowledge applies.

Word Choice Matters

It's incredibly important to key into language that will open your child up (versus close him down). Here's a start to the list of words to use and avoid with your child...at least until his interest in the subject matter is piqued. We encourage you to add more words on either side of the fence.

Use	Avoid
Define	Elaborate
Investigate	Discover
Assemble	Create
Build	Dream
Compute	Imagine
List	Brainstorm
Examine	Explore
Practice	Synthesize
Review	Develop
Watch	Experiment
Detail	Illustrate
Simplify	Analyze
Discuss	Describe

Approaching New Concepts with your ETJ Child

You've probably noticed that your child has a unique gift for standards-based decision-making. This drive to find order and structure in a chaotic world relates not just to schoolwork, but to creating a precise inner categorization of principles against which he can systematically evaluate all decisions.

Because extraverted thinkers like your child want most to achieve goals or come to a definitive conclusion, he will try to systematize procedures to achieve equality when dealing with situations and individuals. Your child wants to know that he has thoroughly analyzed all the variables so that anyone else attempting the same thing in the same way will achieve the same result. What he needs most—particularly when approaching new concepts—is help understanding the relationships and potential contingencies required to make effective decisions. Your child's main drive is to transform individual facts into a clear end goal.

Is It Measurable & Quantifiable?

Your child's learning strength *and weakness* lie in being able to create a streamlined yes/no decision tree. To your child, if an exception needs to be made to a rule, the rule itself needs to be changed. Subjective or qualitative measures of success take a back seat to pure right and wrong answers.

By first talking about how you and the teacher will evaluate success in the class, your child will be able to apply these measures to their assignments. What can be particularly helpful for extraverted thinkers like your child in particular, is to request a rubric from the teacher—both for individual assignments and for the term as a whole—so that you and your child understand the precise criteria against which he will be evaluated. You can find sample rubrics on Kidzmet's printable template CD.

Neuroscientists have recently discovered that dopamine is the brain chemical that causes us to seek out, search and want. Your child craves interaction and discussion in order to seek out new information or search for new perspectives—it not only gives him new insights, but allows him to debate those insights with others. In order to get your child really excited about a subject, talk to him about it before sending him into the "solo zone" to finish homework. Even if he doesn't really seem to be listening to what you say, your role as a sounding board helps him to think things through. If you're not available for this conversation, recruit your spouse or a close relative, or plan study groups with other extraverts in your child's class.

Outcome Oriented & Opinionated

Your child appreciates an agenda for the day, term

or year much more than other personality types. Knowing what's expected on what timeline and how it will be objectively evaluated will help your child back into the decision tree and timeline required to earn a high mark. A typical extraverted thinker like your child strives for competence in every arena.

Even if your child doesn't know a lot about a topic, chances are he will voice an opinion about it. This opinion is typically meant to open a debate about the subject matter, so that your child can establish the rules and boundaries that apply to the scenario. Be aware that extraverted thinkers like your child find paradoxes more challenging to wrap their heads around than most temperament types. In his mind, there's no way that two seemingly contradictory conclusions can both be true.

YOUR CHILD IS A LINEAR LEARNER

It's important to help your child develop a step-by-step approach to concept understanding.

One technique that can work particularly well is to teach him to skim a paragraph or passage once, then go back and highlight, underline or make note of the key parts of the paragraph. Repeat this process until the required reading is complete, then assemble the detail building blocks he has identified into a more general idea.

In this way, your child will fill in the puzzle pieces in a way that feels like a tried-and-true order. And, as I'm sure you've noticed in other aspects of your child's life, extraverted thinkers are more enthusiastic about tasks when they can be approached systematically.

For your child, whatever you can do to make tackling new tasks more logical, structured and organized will reap huge dividends.

If your child is struggling, help him to identify the key details required for understanding, or show him a formula, process or procedure to follow. Map out an approach to take, then identify priorities and create a structure he can follow to achieve the desired outcome.

Word Choice Matters

It's incredibly important to key into language that will open your child up (versus close him down). Here's a start to the list of words to use and avoid with your child...at least until his interest in the subject matter is piqued.

Use	Avoid
Critique	Express
Debate	Cooperate
Generate	Contribute
Synthesize	Assist
Examine	Suggest
Compute	Share
Systematize	Help
Categorize	Clarify
Fix	Request
Assemble	Translate
Order	Survey
Determine	Reflect
Assess	Feel

Approaching New Concepts with your IFP Child

You've probably noticed that your child has a unique gift for seeing the best in people. This compassion and concern relates not just to living beings, but also to deeply held values, beliefs and ideals—even if not always openly expressed or in alignment with cultural norms.

Because introverted feelers like your child want most to maintain harmony, he will make choices about learning new concepts that keep the peace with his study groups, peers, teachers and parents... especially if those individuals have taken the time to get to know him on a personal level. The good news is that this typically means that your child will do his best for both you and his teachers...particularly if a caring and warm personal relationship has been established. What he needs most—particularly when approaching new concepts—is affirmation from you and his teachers that he's on the right track.

Taking Things Personally

Your child's learning strength *and weakness* lies in his desire to align learning with his internal sense of values. By sharing how the new concept can benefit your child personally, or how it can help people in general, your child will be much more open to learning more.

In order to get your child really excited about a subject, talk to your child one-on-one about it after he has had some uninterrupted time in the "solo zone." He needs this time for private consideration and quiet reflection of new concepts. Be aware that he also needs this time to see whether his understanding of the concept feels right before discussing it. If he's not "getting it," try relating firsthand experiences of how you have seen the concept in action.

The most important part is to allow for reflection, which allows your child to both construct and reconstruct his understanding of the material. After he reflects, talk through the parallels he has drawn, then encourage him to once again reflect on his now deeper understanding. Realize that if your child takes a definitive stand on a subject, he will not feel it is open for debate, so you may again need to draw your own parallels to similar situations. This will help him see the other side of the coin.

This reflect → discuss → reflect learning progression resonates strongly for parents who are also introverts, but for extraverted parents can seem just...well... wrong. Introverts by nature prefer uninterrupted time to reflect on new information before discussing it. Introverts also won't typically voice a thought or opinion unless they're sure it's correct, and can find "layered" conversations (the kind with lots of interruptions, preferred by extraverts) jarring.

Participating in layered conversations is particularly

frustrating for introverted feelers like your child

because he has a greater tendency than most

personality types to take interruptions personally.

What Do You Mean, Take Emotion Out of the Equation?

Because your child's understandings need to "feel

right" to him, introducing new concepts that aren't

aligned with his inner values or core beliefs can be

very uncomfortable for your child. In some cases,

your child may ignore or resist new information

that appears to conflict with his values.

Similarly, if a teacher is too formal or rule-

bound, or belittles students in front of the class,

your child may take his dislike or disdain for

the class or teacher to the point that he feels he

just doesn't like the subject itself—a permanent

perspective versus a temporary circumstance.

A LEARNING DANCE VS. DASH

It's important to allow your child to meander

through material instead of demanding that

he follow a step-by-step approach.

One technique that can work particularly well

is to teach your child to dig into each aspect of

the concept or chapter, starting with whatever

aspect piques his interest most, then talk about

how that aspect fits into his own experiences.

In this way, your child will fill in the puzzle pieces

in a way that either intrigues or makes most

sense to him. And, as I'm sure you've noticed

in other aspects of your child's life, introverted

feelers are more enthusiastic about tasks when

they can relate them to personal experience.

For your child, whatever you can do to make new concepts personally significant will help "chunk" the new knowledge in a way that makes most sense to him, which has been shown in numerous studies to aid retention.

WORD CHOICE MATTERS

It's incredibly important to key into language that will open your child up (versus close him down). Here's a start to the list of words to use and avoid with your child...at least until his interest in the subject matter is piqued.

USE	AVOID
Express	Critique
Cooperate	Debate
Contribute	Generate
Assist	Synthesize
Suggest	Examine
Share	Compute
Help	Systematize
Clarify	Categorize
Request	Fix
Translate	Assemble
Survey	Order
Reflect	Determine
Feel	Assess

Approaching New Concepts with your INJ Child

You've probably noticed that your child has a unique gift for unearthing significance and meaning from the seemingly ordinary patterns and themes the rest of us perceive in our environments.

Because your child uses hunches and intuition as a guide for understanding, introducing new concepts is tantalizing because of the clues it can provide to your child about the nature of life itself. The challenge is keeping your child grounded in reality long enough to grasp the details or tried-and-true process required by his teachers. This is further confounded by your child's tendency to question—or even disregard—authority figures. If you want to see your child dive headlong into a subject, just tell him that what he is attempting cannot be done.

The "why," "how," and "what if" questions that come along with understanding new concepts is the "seeking" dopamine rush that your child enjoys most. If you stay too long in the concrete details of what is already known or what is in the past, you may see his eyes glaze over.

That's Dope!

Neuroscientists have recently discovered that the brain chemical dopamine causes us to seek out, search and want. In order to get your child really excited about a subject, talk to him about it *after* he has had some time in the "solo zone" with his ideas and quiet reflection on his homework. Or, if you're not available for this conversation, recruit your spouse or a close relative.

The most important part is to allow for this reflection, which allows your child to both construct and reconstruct his understanding of the material. After this reflection process, talk through the parallels your child has drawn, then encourage him once again to reflect on his now deeper understanding of the subject. The flipped classroom that's talked about so much these days in the media is tailor-made for introverts like your child.

This reflect → discuss → reflect learning progression resonates strongly for parents who are also introverts, but for extraverted parents can seem just...well... wrong. Introverts by nature prefer to reflect on new information first before discussing it. Introverts also won't typically voice a thought or opinion unless they're sure it's correct. Extraverts, on the other hand, talk their way to understanding, so in most cases what they say is not necessarily a complete or final thought.

Even the ways in which conversation is structured is different for introverts. Introverted intuitives like your child often won't volunteer a perspective unless they've been explicitly asked for it and may not provide much input or feedback during group discussions. But they will reveal brilliant—though most likely abstract—insights after taking time to absorb the various perspectives they've heard.

Inspired Impressionists

Your child's learning strength lies in thinking outside the box. Your child is passionate about figuring out how everything fits into the big picture. In the grand scheme of things, your child is an impressionist in every sense of the word. So be sure to avoid staying in facts or tried-and-true for too long at the outset; instead, paint the broad strokes of the subject first and then fill in the details.

Your child will most likely need your help to make sure important details are not glossed over and that he stays on task rather than heading off on a tangent. If he starts to go off on a tangent, pull him back in with questions like, "What about X in this scenario?"

LEARNING DETECTIVE

It's important to allow your child to dictate the path
he takes toward understanding. Think of him like a
learning detective finding relevant clues along the
way to solving the mystery. For your child, flashes
of insight and inspiration will be remembered
far better and longer than routine tasks.

One technique that can work particularly well is to
teach your child to keep the chapter wrap-up a "secret,"
then have him take notes on what he believes to be the
important pieces of understanding within the chapter.
Finally, see how closely his intuition matched the reality.

In this way, your child will skim, scan and summarize
in an attempt to predict an outcome. And, as
I'm sure you've noticed in other aspects of your
child's life, he feels most gratified when things
turn out the way he predicted they would.

WORD CHOICE MATTERS

It's incredibly important to key into language that will open your child up (versus close him down). Here's a start to the list of words to use and avoid with your child...at least until his interest in the subject matter is piqued.

USE	AVOID
Elaborate	Define
Discover	Investigate
Create	Assemble
Dream	Build
Imagine	Compute
Brainstorm	List
Explore	Examine
Synthesize	Practice
Develop	Review
Experiment	Watch
Illustrate	Detail
Analyze	Simplify
Describe	Discuss

Approaching New Concepts with your ISJ Child

You've probably noticed that your child has a unique gift for reliving experiences and comparing those experiences to what is happening in the present.

Because your child uses his previous experiences as a guide for present understanding, introducing new concepts without a foundation can be very uncomfortable for your child. Luckily, when you approach new concepts in a way that embraces your child's nature, the dopamine rush he experiences will keep him coming back for more learning because his past learning experiences were positive.

THAT'S DOPE!

Neuroscientists have recently discovered that the brain chemical dopamine causes us to seek out, search and want. In order to get your child really excited about a subject, talk to him about it *after* he has had some time in the "solo zone" with his ideas and quiet reflection on his homework. Or, if you're not available for this conversation, recruit your spouse or a close relative.

The most important part is to allow for this reflection, which allows your child to both construct and reconstruct his understanding of the material. After this reflection process, talk through the parallels your child has drawn, then encourage him once again to reflect on his now deeper understanding of the subject. The flipped classroom that's talked about so much these days in the media is tailor-made for introverts like your child.

This reflect → discuss → reflect learning progression resonates strongly for parents who are also introverts, but for extraverted parents can seem just...well... wrong. Introverts by nature prefer to reflect on new information first before discussing it. Introverts also won't typically voice a thought or opinion unless they're sure it's correct. Extraverts, on the other hand, talk their way to understanding, so in most cases what they say is not necessarily a complete or final thought.

Even the ways in which conversation is structured is different for introverts. Introverts often won't volunteer a perspective unless they've been explicitly asked for it and may not provide much input or feedback during group discussions, but will reveal brilliant insights after taking time to absorb the various perspectives they've heard.

JUST THE FACTS, MA'AM...AT LEAST IN THE BEGINNING

Your child's learning strength lies in grasping facts and details versus more general concepts. Your child first wants to answer the question "What specifically do I need to learn?" or "How precisely will this assignment be graded?" before diving in. In the grand scheme of things, your child prefers to be more of a tree trimmer than a forest ranger. So be sure to avoid using abstract concepts to "paint the big picture" of the subject in the beginning, but instead start with the facts— ideally information he takes in with his five senses.

Your child will most likely need your help during the initial phase of projects to establish precisely what is expected of him by the instructor and work through an attack plan.

Your Child is a Linear Learner

It's important to help your child develop a step-by-step approach to concept understanding.

One technique that can work particularly well is to teach him to skim a paragraph or passage once, then go back and highlight, underline or make note of the key parts of the paragraph. Repeat this process until the required

73

reading is complete, then assemble the building block detail he has identified into a more general idea.

In this way, your child will fill in the puzzle pieces in a way that feels like a tried-and-true order. And, as I'm sure you've noticed in other aspects of your child's life, introverted sensors are more enthusiastic about tasks when they can approach them methodically.

For your child, whatever you can do to make new concepts tangible, concrete or sensorial will reap huge dividends.

Do your best not to interrupt your child during homework and allow him to tackle the new knowledge methodically instead of jumping around. If your child is struggling, help him to identify the key details required for understanding or show him a formula, process or procedure to follow. Don't talk about which other aspects of life in which this new knowledge applies until he feels he has got a solid foundational understanding of the core concept.

WORD CHOICE MATTERS

It's incredibly important to key into language that will open your child up (versus close him down). Here's a start to the list of words to use and avoid with your child...at least until his interest in the subject matter is piqued.

USE	AVOID
Define	Elaborate
Investigate	Discover
Assemble	Create
Build	Dream
List	Imagine
Examine	Brainstorm
Practice	Explore
Review	Synthesize
Observe	Develop
Detail	Experiment
Simplify	Illustrate
Discuss	Analyze

Approaching New Concepts with your ITP Child

You've probably noticed that your child has a unique gift for weighing the pros and cons of a decision and arriving at the most logical conclusions. This logical analysis and ability to find both flaws and fixes relates not just to schoolwork, but to creating a precise inner categorization of principles against which he can systematically evaluate all decisions.

Because introverted thinkers like your child want most to maintain internal order and precision, he will use his internal classifications to deal with events and refine ideas. Your child wants to know exactly how everything works and relates best to people who he believes to be both fair and truthful. What he needs most—particularly when approaching new concepts—is help dispelling anxiety or frustration when what he expected to happen is different than what occurred...especially when he

believes the logic upon which he relied on to come

to the conclusion is straightforward or undeniable.

Your child's need to flesh out his inner decision tree

will often result in an avalanche of questions in an

area he doesn't feel he understands thoroughly yet.

Is It Logical & Quantifiable?

Your child's learning strength and weakness lie in

being able to distill down decisions to the most logical

choice. That being said, he may have more difficulty

listening or staying open to new information rather

than finding ways to challenge the new idea.

By first talking about any assumptions required for

understanding a new concept, and then sharing the

cause-and-effect relationships, your child will be

able to more quickly grasp the new knowledge.

In order to get your child really excited about a subject,

talk to your child about why the new concept is credible

and reliable after he has had some uninterrupted

time in the "solo zone." He needs this time for private

consideration and quiet reflection of new concepts.

Be aware that he also needs this time to evaluate

whether his understanding of the concept passes his

internal analysis of its logic and reason. If he's not

"getting it," try relating it to other concepts he knows

that follow similar patterns. Realize that if your child

takes an incorrect stand on a subject, he will need

you to help him reveal additional assumptions or

biases that make his initial take inaccurate. Precise

corrective feedback is necessary for him to expand

his internal framework for understanding.

This reflect → discuss → reflect learning progression

resonates strongly for parents who are also introverts,

but for extroverted parents can seem just...well...

wrong. Introverts by nature prefer uninterrupted time

to reflect on new information before discussing it.

Introverts also won't typically voice a thought or opinion

unless they're sure it's correct, and can find "layered"

conversations (the kind with lots of interruptions,

preferred by extroverts) jarring. To your child, layered

conversations feel like micro-management. Your child

also is incredibly good at playing devil's advocate

and can get frustrated or impatient if he feels you

aren't thoroughly thinking the concept through.

FITTING THE FRAMEWORK

Be aware that your child's understandings are much

like today's supercomputers, with a complex set of if/

then statements that lead him to logical conclusions, so

introducing new concepts without a solid foundation

can be very uncomfortable for your child. In some

cases, your child may ignore or resist new information

that appears to conflict with his internal filters.

A Learning Dance vs. Dash

It's important to allow your child to meander through material instead of demanding that he follow a step-by-step approach.

One technique that can work particularly well is to teach your child to dig into each aspect of the concept or chapter, starting with whatever aspect piques his interest most, then talk about how that aspect logically fits into his understanding.

In this way, your child will fill in the puzzle pieces in the way that makes most sense to him and allows him do some out-of-the-box thinking that comes so naturally to him. For your child, whatever you can do to make new concepts logically relevant will help him sift through and "chunk" the new knowledge in a way that makes most sense to him, which has been shown in numerous studies to aid retention.

WORD CHOICE MATTERS

It's incredibly important to key into language that will open your child up (versus close him down). Here's a start to the list of words to use and avoid with your child...at least until his interest in the subject matter is piqued.

USE	AVOID
Critique	Express
Debate	Cooperate
Generate	Contribute
Synthesize	Assist
Examine	Suggest
Compute	Share
Systematize	Help
Categorize	Clarify
Fix	Request
Assemble	Translate
Order	Survey
Determine	Reflect
Assess	Feel

Note Taking and "Filing" Knowledge

"It's a remarkable feature of our educational system that we give students so much stuff to learn and rarely tell them how to go about learning that stuff. Learners tend to think of 'how do I get all this stuff into my head?' and they don't spend much time considering how they will get all of that stuff back out of their heads when the time comes to retrieve it."

~Purdue University psychologist Jeffrey D. Karpicke

You've probably seen the opposite of this three wise monkeys image numerous times. In fact, it's been around for at least 400 years. Learning styles reflect a similar concept. But, contrary to popular belief, learning styles aren't so much a way to identify how to put things *in* into your mind, but more of a **filing system** to help you *retrieve* things you've learned as quickly as possible. Your child will still need to have a well-rounded understanding of the subject matter, which means absorbing it through visual, auditory and kinesthetic modalities whenever possible...but he can use his preferred "shorthand" to file it in a way that he can pull it out as quickly and effortlessly as possible.

Why is this important? Most tests (including the standardized, high-stakes variety) are timed. So every edge you can give your child to help pull out the knowledge he has worked so hard to learn is important.

Think back on your last vacation. What do you remember first? What you saw? What you heard? What you felt or did? You took in memories through all your senses, but one sense resurfaced fastest. Similarly, your child will remember one aspect of a concept first/fastest. Circle the order in which your child prefers each filing preference on each of the next three pages. (This information is also included on your child's Kidzmet® preference profile, based on their answers.) The lists will tell you which techniques and tactics work best for each filing preference.

Your Child Prefers to File Knowledge by *Doing*

MOST   AVERAGE   LEAST

- Have your child work through in-class assignments (e.g., math problems) on a sliding glass door or mirrored closet door.

- Talk to your child's teacher about allowing him to take notes or diagram lessons on paper as the teacher lectures.

- Allow your child to take movement breaks or stretch every 15 minutes or so while completing homework.

- If you have access to a stationary bike, encourage your child to read homework assignments while riding it, pace while doing test prep, or take a walk when brainstorming an essay or writing assignment.

- Encourage your child to learn the alphabet in sign language, so that he can more easily cement spelling words and mnemonics in memory.

- Use Touch Math to make addition and subtraction tasks easier.

- Use manipulatives like legos or jelly beans to change abstract concepts like 2 + 3 = 5 into concrete tasks (2 jelly beans and 3 jelly beans makes 5 jelly beans).

- Have your child "teach" the concept that the class is learning to you prior to test or quiz day.

Your Child Prefers to File Knowledge by *Seeing*

MOST   AVERAGE   LEAST

- Find videos on YouTube, Khan Academy, TeacherTube, etc., of the concepts he is learning in class so that your child can "see" the lesson again.

- Teach your child to Mind Map, Venn Diagram or timeline concepts. (Examples of these types of graphic organizers can be found at the end of this chapter.)

- Encourage your child to illustrate homework problems to be solved. For instance, if a word problem is "Mary has 3 apples and Suzy takes 2 of them. How many apples does Mary have left?", then have your child draw two stick figures and three apples under one stick figure, then circle two of the apples and draw an arrow to Suzy.

- Talk to your child's teacher about giving him scratch paper during quizzes and tests so that he can diagram or illustrate test questions as necessary.

Your Child Prefers to File Knowledge by *Hearing*

MOST   AVERAGE   LEAST

- Encourage your child to read study materials aloud to help commit the information to memory.

- Talk to your child's teacher about allowing him to record lectures instead of taking notes so that he can dedicate full attention to his predominant learning modality.

- Help your child put conceptual lyrics to rhythms or familiar tunes whenever possible (e.g., Mary Had a Little Lamb for "I before E except after C except when said 'ay' as in neighbor and weigh"). Tools like Flocabulary can be particularly effective in this vein.

- Talk through the "big picture" of an assignment with your child before putting pen to paper.

- Arrange study groups with other students prior to exams and quizzes to allow your child to both hear and talk about the concepts that the test will cover.

- LearningAlly offers a wide array of textbooks as MP3s and can be helpful for auditory learners like your child.

Samples of Graphic Organizers

Here are a few types of graphic organizers. You'll find many more on Kidzmet's template CD.

VENN DIAGRAM

Write down what makes two subjects similar in the parts of the circles that overlap and what makes them different in the parts of the circles that don't overlap.

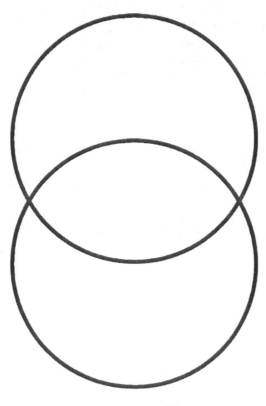

PROBLEM SOLUTION CHART

List potential problems in the left column and

possible solutions in the right column below.

PROBLEMS | SOLUTIONS

STORY SPIDER

Write the central idea on the center circle.

Write the main ideas on the slanted lines

and the details on the horizontal ones.

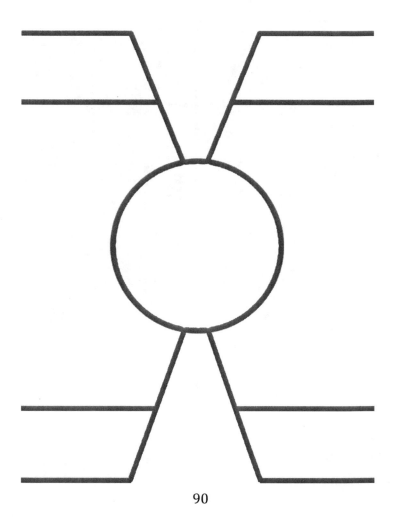

PROJECT TREE

List the central idea on the trunk, the supporting ideas on the branches, and details on the leaves. (Or use post-it notes for leaves.)

Project Timeline

List the aspects of the project to complete in the boxes.

List the number of days you need to complete each

piece on the slanted lines. Make the boxes longer or

shorter depending on how long you believe each task

will take...and whether some of them can overlap.

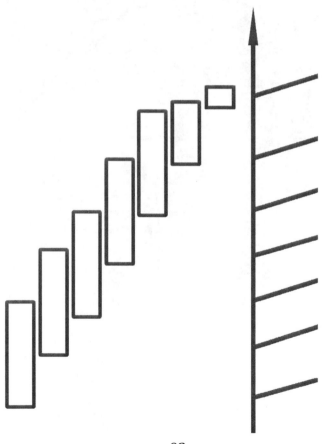

Homework Practice
and Test Prep

"When new information is recognized as related to prior knowledge, learning extends beyond the domain in which it occurred. It is available through transfer to create new predictions and solutions to problems in other areas beyond the classroom or test."

~Mind, Brain & Education: Neuroscience

Implications for the Classroom.

Sousa, D., Willis, J. et. al. (2010)

There once was an archer who could shoot arrows with such accuracy that no one could beat him. One day at the archery field during a demonstration for onlookers, he noticed that one old man did not appear to be impressed.

Only with a slight nod of his head did the old man acknowledge his shots. Dismayed, the archer demanded, "Why are you not impressed by me? Can you do better?" To which the old man replied, "You've gained your skill from persistent practice, that is all."

"How do you know?" balked the archer.

The man put a bottle on the ground and covered its mouth with a washer with a small hole in the middle. He then scooped a ladle of water from a nearby pail, held it high and began to fill the bottle. The onlookers watched with amazement as the old man filled the bottle to the brim without spilling a single drop.

As the crowd began to applaud, the old man said,

"This is nothing special. I can do this because I have

practiced it a lot." And with these words, he left.

Many times we are amazed by how skillful someone is at something—especially when that someone is a friend or classmate. But what we need to remind our kids is that it has taken that person a lot of time, practice, failures, and struggles to make his skill appear effortless… whether that skill is math, soccer, piano or spelling.

Homework Practice & Test Prep for the EFJ Child

When it comes to school work, your child enjoys learning or practicing skills with black and white answers or that he feels confident will please his peers and teachers. On the other hand, he will most likely try to put off assignments in which he is required to take a position which may not rub his peers or teachers the right way. Your child naturally takes on the emotional burdens of others...even if they are just imagined.

The more contentious the subject matter, the more your child will need someone (be it you, a study group or a tutor) to help him talk it out.

As an added bonus, contextualizing new knowledge according to how others feel about it helps your child better "chunk" the information, by grouping

items together in a way that is most meaningful
for him. This chunking process has been shown
to aid retention in numerous studies.

You = Cheerleader

When helping your child with homework, consider
how a cheerleader helps players on the field believe
that they can do it...even when the going gets tough.
Just as your child praises others openly and often,
he also thrives when encouraged or appreciated.

This is the same approach you need to apply to your
child's assignments. Because the teacher has many
students to juggle or may have a Thinking personality
type, he or she may not give your child the validation
he needs to feel secure that he is on the right track. If
your child seems to stall out during homework, motivate
him to press on by emphasizing how proud you will
be of him when he completes it, since extraverted
feelers like your child often will redouble their effort

when they believe external harmony is at stake.

INTERACTIVE TEST PREP

While some kids prefer to prep for tests alone, your child learns best in a more social atmosphere. For this reason, forgoing flash cards for Family Game Night can be an incredibly successful strategy.

Whether you re-purpose Candy Land, Twister or Trivial Pursuit, your child will be willing to practice skills longer when it's social. And you show through your participation in the game that knowing this information is important not only to your child, but also to you and to your family. Board games also provide the opportunity for one-on-one discussion about each topic and the "You can do it! I believe in you!" cheerleading that we discussed earlier, immediately following any errors. Finally, board games tie knowledge to affectivity—or arousing emotion—which has been shown to also aid concept retention...particularly for extraverted feelers like your child. Why? When your child gets an answer correct, he gets closer to winning, which produces a "Yay!" emotion. When he gets an answer wrong, he loses a turn, which produces a "Boo!" emotion.

CEMENTING KNOWLEDGE

The more you give your child *similar* mnemonics (or ways to assist the memory) like rhymes and songs for auditory learners, images and patterns for visual learners, or movements and manipulatives for kinesthetic learners, the more organized his mental filing system will be and, as a result, the faster he will be able to put his finger on required knowledge—something more critical for extraverted feelers than most other personality types.

Homework Practice & Test Prep for the ENP Child

When it comes to school work, your child harnesses an enormous amount of energy to start projects, but his energy seems to vanish as soon as the idea phase is over and it's time to work out the details.

To reinvigorate him, do your best to tie the subject matter at hand to something your child loves to do, and show him how understanding what's being studied can help him accomplish other goals faster or more easily.

As an added bonus, contextualizing new knowledge in this way helps your child better "chunk" the information by grouping items together in a way that is meaningful. This chunking process has been shown to aid retention in numerous studies. Plus, tying seemingly unrelated subjects together in this way embraces your child's preference for the learning dance we discussed in our chapter on approaching new concepts.

FOCUS AND CONCENTRATION

Because focus and concentration is a perpetual challenge for extraverted intuitives like your child, homework and long-term projects can be a considerable source of frustration for parents.

Your child's innate tendency to get sidetracked could easily turn into the root cause for school failures, especially given how kids like him loathe routine or practicing the same approach over and over.

While homework is supposed to take 10 minutes per grade, you may need to work at your child's ability to focus for long periods of time.

If your child seems to get distracted easily, time how long his focus window lasts early in the school year—or

even start this process over the summer—and break
homework up into individual subjects, then work on
stretching focus time slowly, by only a minute per grade
level per week. (E.g., five minutes a week for a fifth
grader versus two minutes a week for a second grader.)

Play-Based Test Prep

While some kids prefer to separate work and play,
perceivers like your child would rather combine work
and play. For this reason, it's best to forgo the flashcards
and turn weekly test prep night into Family Game Night.

Whether you re-purpose Candy Land, Twister or
Trivial Pursuit, your child will be willing to practice
skills longer in the context of a game. Board games
also provide the opportunity for discussion about
each topic that extraverts like your child need to
deepen and cement understanding. Finally, board
games tie knowledge to affectivity—or arousing
emotion—which has been shown to also aid concept

retention. Why? When your child gets an answer correct, he gets closer to winning, which produces a "Yay!" emotion. When he gets an answer wrong, he loses a turn, which produces a "Boo!" emotion.

Because of your child's natural tendency to gloss over specific facts and details, make sure you remind him to key into the details.

Homework Practice & Test Prep for the ESP Child

When it comes to school work, your child enjoys practicing skills in which he feels adept or assignments which he can immediately put into practice, but his energy will seem to vanish during a more abstract idea phase or if you talk about how he'll need the knowledge "someday."

To reinvigorate him, do your best to illustrate a practical purpose for the lesson and give concrete examples of why or how this knowledge is needed for daily life.

As an added bonus, contextualizing new knowledge in this way helps your child better "chunk" the information by grouping items together in a way that is meaningful. This chunking process has been shown in numerous studies to aid retention.

Homework GPS

When helping your child with homework, consider how you give someone directions to a location they've never been before. You not only provide turn-by-turn directions, but you'll often identify landmarks along the way to ensure he stays on the right path.

This is the same approach you need to help your child apply to assignments. Often, the teacher will provide just the destination. If your child comes home with this kind of assignment, help your child to outline the lesson, then figure out a step-by-step approach for completion.

Teacher Translation

You may run into the opposite problem with other teachers who provide lengthy, abstract directions which can be overwhelming to your child. If this is the case, help your child pick out the key words that will help him "translate" directions into something clear, concise and concrete from which he can work.

PLAY-BASED TEST PREP

While some kids prefer to separate work and play, perceivers like your child would rather combine work and play. For this reason, it's best to forgo the flashcards and turn weekly test prep night into Family Game Night.

Whether you re-purpose Candy Land, Twister or Trivial Pursuit, your child will be willing to practice skills longer in the context of a game. Board games also provide the opportunity for discussion about each topic that extraverts like your child need to deepen and cement understanding. Finally, board games tie knowledge to affectivity—or arousing emotion—which has been shown to also aid concept retention. Why? When your child gets an answer correct, he gets closer to winning, which produces a "Yay!" emotion. When he gets an answer wrong, he loses a turn, which produces a "Boo!" emotion.

Because of your child's natural tendency to not see the forest for the trees, make sure you remind him to also look at the big picture.

Homework Practice & Test Prep for the ETJ Child

When it comes to school work, your child enjoys organizing information in ways that others can understand and put it into practice, but gets frustrated in more unstructured or subjective classes.

To reinvigorate him, do your best to illustrate how he can bring order to the chaos by talking with the teacher at the beginning of each term, to develop an outline or rubric for evaluation and prepare a class "plan of attack" that will insure a successful outcome.

PRIOR PLANNING PREVENTS POOR PERFORMANCE...MOST OF THE TIME

Extraverted thinkers like your child revel in crossing items off of to-do lists and enjoy the planning process of assignments. However, when an unanticipated wrench gets thrown into the works, your child may struggle with how and when he will accomplish upcoming assignments.

When something unexpected comes up, help your child develop prioritized contingency plans that will help him get the assignment done on time with a good grade. Investing in a tool or software product like Microsoft Project can help simplify this process.

PROJECT-BASED TEST PREP

While some kids prefer to combine work and play, judgers like your child would rather separate them. For this reason, take each class syllabus at the beginning of the term and pencil in time on the calendar for flashcard-based test-prep, and for study groups with other results-oriented kids who like to think out loud

TEST PREP OVER TIME

While some kids prefer to combine work and play and thrive on deadlines, judgers like your child would rather separate work from play and follow a slow-and-steady-wins-the-race approach. Additionally, for your child, a return to the familiar is more comfortable than trying out a new tactic. For this reason, it's best to dedicate a chunk of time to test prep at the beginning of each night's homework and use a study method that has worked well for your child in the past.

Whether you choose to have your child re-read his notes from each class for 10-20 minutes each evening or create flashcards from the day's notes, your child will benefit from reviewing the material within 24 hours of hearing it, which has been shown in studies to increase retention by almost 60%. It will also give your child the chance to uncover anything confusing in his notes and give him the opportunity to clarify any misunderstandings with the teacher prior to the test.

Because of your child's natural tendency to focus

on the black-and-white and cause-and-effect

aspects of lessons, make sure you also talk with

him about the more objective, shades-of-gray

themes of the lesson so that he can form a more

complete picture in his mental filing system.

Homework Practice & Test Prep for the IFP Child

When it comes to school work, your child enjoys practicing skills which he feels have a human or personal impact, but his energy will seem to vanish during more logic-based tasks.

To reinvigorate him, do your best to illustrate a personal purpose for the lesson and give concrete examples of why or how this knowledge impacts his daily life or the lives of those he cares about.

As an added bonus, contextualizing new knowledge in this way helps your child better "chunk" the information by grouping items together in a way that is meaningful.

You = Cheerleader

When helping your child with homework, consider

how a cheerleader helps players on the field believe that they can do it...even when the going gets tough.

TEACHER TRANSLATION

This is the same approach you need to apply to your child's assignments. Because the teacher has many students to juggle or may have a Thinking personality type, he or she may not give your child the validation he needs to feel secure that he is on the right track. If your child seems to stall out during homework, motivate him to press on by tying an aspiration to the assignment, since introverted feelers like your child often will redouble their effort when working on an assignment they believe in.

PLAY-BASED TEST PREP

While some kids prefer to separate work and play, perceivers like your child would rather combine work and play. For this reason, it's best to forgo the flashcards and turn weekly test-prep night into Family Game Night.

Whether you re-purpose Candy Land, Twister or Trivial Pursuit, your child will be willing to practice skills longer in the context of a game. Board games also provide the opportunity for one-on-one discussion about each topic and the "You can do it! I believe in you!" cheerleading that we discussed earlier, immediately following any errors. Finally, board games tie knowledge to affectivity—or arousing emotion—which has been shown to also aid concept retention...particularly for introverted feelers like your child. Why? When your child gets a correct answer, he gets closer to winning, which produces a "Yay!" emotion. When he gets an answer wrong, he loses a turn, which produces a "Boo!" emotion.

Homework Practice & Test Prep for the INJ Child

When it comes to school work, your child enjoys theoretical discussions or strategic thinking, but his energy seems to vanish during more routine tasks, or if limitations or constraints are put on an assignment.

To reinvigorate your child, encourage him to talk about the "butterfly effect" of the lesson or allow him some time to think about how his new understanding might be applied in other, as yet undiscovered areas. (Don't tell your child where else it applies—allow him to make the discoveries on his own!)

As an added bonus, allowing your child to find his own ways to contextualize this new knowledge will help him "chunk" the information better, i.e., group items together in a way that he finds meaningful. This chunking process has been shown to aid retention in numerous studies.

THROW OUT THE RULE BOOK

When helping your child with homework, remember
that he believes that everything can be improved,
even your, or his teacher's, opinion of the "best"
way to approach homework problems! However,
it's important to remind your child that the teacher
needs him to show his work, so that the teacher can
understand how he came to the result. If necessary,
have him prove his system by working it out using a
traditional approach and achieving the same result.

This is the same approach your child should apply
to long-term assignments, so you need to guide
him in that direction. Often, your child will forget
to include the concrete details that led to his
conclusion, and may not even remember why or
how he got there in the first place. Help him to fill in
the blanks by encouraging him to mentally retrace

his steps, and to include the insights that led to his assumptions in the piece he turns in to the teacher.

TEACHER TRANSLATION

You may run into challenges, as well, with other teachers who provide lengthy, step-by-step instructions with many interim due dates. If this is the case, help your child deduce the theme of the teacher's directions that will help him "translate" directions into something more abstract. In other words, something to which he can apply a more creative approach. Just make sure your child checks with the teacher ahead of time to make sure the approach he plans to take is acceptable!

TEST PREP OVER TIME

While some kids prefer to combine work and play and thrive on deadlines, judgers like your child would rather separate work from play and use a slow-and-steady-wins-the-race approach.

Since introverted intuitives like your child find listening carefully for a long time challenging, have him take notes in Q&A or pop quiz format, then quiz him on random material from the chapter and from his notes. Not only will your child benefit from reviewing the material within 24 hours of hearing it—which has been shown in studies to increase retention by almost 60%—it will also give your child the chance to uncover anything confusing in his notes and clarify any misunderstandings with the teacher prior to the test.

Because of your child's natural tendency to gloss over specific facts and details, make sure you also talk with him about the minutiae of the lesson. In this way, he can paint a more realistic mental picture of the material rather than one that's fuzzy on details that are likely to be on the exam.

Homework Practice & Test Prep for the ISJ Child

When it comes to school work, your child enjoys practicing skills in which he feels adept or assignments which he can immediately put into practice, but his energy will seem to vanish during a more abstract idea phase or if you talk about how he'll need the knowledge "someday."

To reinvigorate him, do your best to illustrate a practical purpose for the lesson and give concrete examples of why or how this knowledge is needed or helpful in his daily life.

As an added bonus, contextualizing new knowledge in this way helps your child better "chunk" the information by grouping items together in a way that is meaningful. This chunking process has been shown in numerous studies to aid retention.

Homework GPS

When helping your child with homework, consider how you give someone directions to a location they've never been before. You not only provide turn-by-turn directions, but you'll often identify landmarks along the way to ensure he stays on the right path.

This is the same approach you need to help your child apply to assignments. Often, the teacher will provide just the destination. If your child comes home with this kind of assignment, help him to outline the lesson, then figure out a step-by-step approach for completion.

Teacher Translation

You may run into the opposite problem with other teachers who provide lengthy, abstract directions which can be overwhelming to your child. If this is the case, help your child pick out the key words that will help him "translate" directions into something clear, concise and concrete from which he can work.

TEST PREP OVER TIME

While some kids prefer to combine work and play and thrive on deadlines, judgers like your child would rather separate work from play and follow a slow-and-steady-wins-the-race approach. Additionally, for your child, a return to the familiar is more comfortable than trying out a new tactic. For this reason, it's best to dedicate a chunk of time to test prep at the beginning of each night's homework and use a study method that has worked well for your child in the past.

Whether you choose to have your child re-read his notes from each class for 10-20 minutes each evening or create flashcards from the day's notes, he will benefit from reviewing the material within 24 hours of hearing it, which has shown in studies to increase retention by almost 60%. It will also give your child the chance to uncover anything confusing in his

notes and give him the opportunity to clarify any

misunderstandings with the teacher prior to the test.

Because of your child's natural tendency to focus

on specific facts and details, make sure you also

talk with him about the over-arching themes of

the lesson so that he can develop a more complete

understanding in his mental filing system.

Homework Practice & Test Prep for the ITP Child

When it comes to school work, your child enjoys practicing skills which he feels have a dependable cause-and-effect nature, but his energy will seem to vanish during more subjective tasks.

To reinvigorate him, do your best to illustrate how he can filter down the emotional aspects into a logical bias or assumption so that he can make the shades of gray appear more black-and-white. As an added bonus, helping your child understand how to filter values-based information will help not only improve his efforts in school, but also help him relate to peers and teachers more effectively.

YOU= CRITIC

When helping your child with homework, consider how

a critic distills down the review of a book or movie to a succinct analysis of exactly where it went wrong.

This is the same approach you need to apply to your child's assignments. Because the teacher has many students to juggle or may have a Feeling personality type, he or she may not give your child the specific corrections he needs to understand where he went wrong so he can avoid the same misstep in the future. If your child seems to stall out during homework, motivate him to press on by helping him filter out data that doesn't matter or talk about how this knowledge is important in the real world, since introverted thinkers like your child often will redouble their effort when working on an assignment that has real world implications.

If a teacher expects your child to do things "just because" without thoroughly explaining the underlying logic...or the teacher gets frustrated by his "Question Authority" approach to learning, your child may start to believe that the teacher is not a credible or competent subject area expert and may stop trying to assimilate new knowledge because he doesn't know what new data to filter out or place in a permanent framework. If this is the case, encourage him to find other, more renowned sources of knowledge in the domain...be they textbooks, online resources, peers or tutors.

PROJECT-BASED TEST PREP

While some kids prefer to separate work and play, perceivers like your child would rather combine work and play. For this reason, it's best to forgo the flashcards and turn weekly test-prep night into Family Game Night.

Whether you re-purpose Candy Land, Twister or Trivial Pursuit, your child will be willing to practice skills longer in the context of a game. Board games also provide the opportunity for the friendly competition and black-and-white answers that introverted thinkers like your child relish, as well as quick, targeted feedback when he answers incorrectly.

Group Learning

"In dealing with people, when we keep their type in mind, we are respecting not only their abstract right to develop along lines of their own choosing, but also the importance of qualities they have developed by making that choice."

~MBTI Manual

Briggs Myers, Isabel, McCaulley, Mary H., Quenk,

Naomi L., & Hammer, Allen L. (1998)

A *fox once struck a deal with a lion, on the pretense of helping each other to dine like kings. Each undertook a role that fully utilized his own nature and strengths. When the fox discovered and pointed out their prey, the lion pounced on it and killed it. The fox soon began to think that he could be equally as successful going it alone, and said that he would no longer team up with the lion, but would capture prey on his own.*

The next day he attempted to snatch a lamb from the fold, but instead fell prey to the huntsman and his hounds.

Combining forces can yield better results for all involved.

If you are a part of an organization or company, you have had an opportunity to experience how many individuals' talents and energies can combine to create something much more powerful than an individual who goes it alone.

But in order to truly get the best result, each individual involved must have the opportunity to play to his or her strengths and talents. For instance, using a trained artist as an accountant within an organization while the "numbers guy" designs ads will not be nearly as successful as it could have been had the organization flopped the roles. In the same way, a born artist trained as an accountant won't be as effective or energized analyzing the books as a born statistician would be.

Group learning can be enormously powerful for kids, but it needs to be approached in a similar way. Just as we discussed in our chapter on approaching new concepts, kids are all coming at the conceptual elephant from different angles. They first need peer acknowledgement that their perception is accurate. Then, they need to practice and cement their knowledge and expand their understanding of the concept. Finally, they need to get a more holistic view of how this concept fits into the larger puzzle.

One way to look at this is to think of knowledge not as a wall that every child adds to from the ground up in an identical way, but as a Rubik's Cube with the concept at the very center of the cube that expands brick by brick in three dimensions. How kids choose to build that cube depends on their innate world view. If they don't get acknowledgement that their initial block of understanding is accurate, they won't be able to put this understanding in the context of the bigger picture as quickly or successfully.

Just as there are people types you are drawn to in romantic relationships, friends you click with better than others, and certain work colleagues that bring out your best, your child's ideal learning and study groups will also be compatible ones. At the end of each of the following sections for each type of learner, you'll see a wheel chart of which types of students are best to invite for study groups at different stages of learning.

If you're not sure what type each student is, you can ask their parents to have them complete the free Kidzmet® preference profile, then let you know the results. The most effective study groups will NOT necessarily be the kids your child naturally gravitates toward hanging out with...but they learn in compatible ways.

Group Learning for an EFJ Child

As an extravert, your child thrives in group discussions.
However, as a feeler, you'll need to keep close tabs on
your child's study groups. They need to stay focused
on the assignment at hand and not on challenges or
situations currently confronting their classmates
or families. You might also want to help your child
develop a checklist for study groups you host at your
house, because it's easy for him to shift focus away
from homework to host, as social tasks like invitations,
snacks and seating arrangements become first priority.

At an intro level, you'll want to help your child plan
study groups that understand the human side of
things. You will need to work with your child on
feeling comfortable giving and receiving constructive
criticism, as he will be likely to agree with others
in the group just for the sake of harmony, and will
often choose tact over truth to avoid clashes.

One of the best ways to use a study group with your child is to get the students together during each project phase to be cheerleaders for each other, as this belief in each other can improve a feeling group's performance across the board. This said, in long-term assignments, it's absolutely vital for your child to include a broader range of personality types, since your child will need both a "hater" and a motivator in order to complete a truly polished final product...even if the conflict is initially upsetting.

Be on the lookout during group projects for your child volunteering to take on the bulk of the work. Extraverted feelers like your child not only have a hard time saying no, they also have a hard time accepting that they can't do it all.

Your Child's Optimal Study Buddies

The wheel below shows which temperaments

work best with your child at intro (seed), practice

(sprout) and growth (grass) phases of learning.

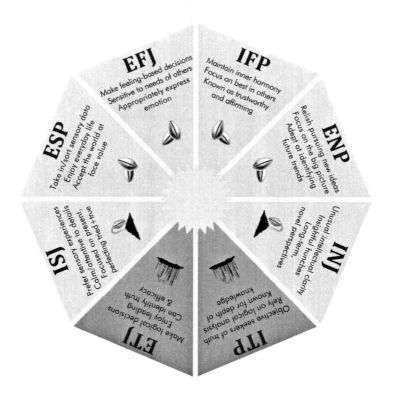

Group Learning for an ENP Child

As an extravert, your child learns well from study groups, since verbalizing thoughts helps him process questions, problems, or discussions more effectively. Study groups also give your child a compelling external reason for studying—not just because it's something he "has to do". You'll also find that your child will be more inclined to work on projects for a longer time in teams than alone.

At an intro level, you'll want to help your child plan study groups that talk things out or also tend to be more focused on possibilities than realities.

At a practice stage, expect to have a group that combines work and play. This group will be flexible and tolerant of changing agendas. You can also expect this group to be energized by deadlines.

Once it's time to get down to business on completing a challenging assignment, however, your child needs a quiet, distraction-free space in which to concentrate...which means it's time for the study group to disband for the night.

YOUR CHILD'S OPTIMAL STUDY BUDDIES

The wheel below shows which temperaments work best with your child at intro (seed), practice (sprout) and growth (grass) phases of learning.

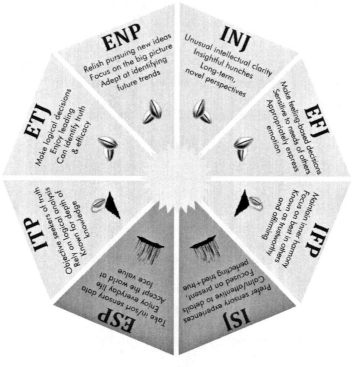

Group Learning for an ESP Child

As an extravert, your child learns well from study groups, since verbalizing thoughts helps him process questions, problems, or discussions more effectively. Study groups also give your child a compelling external reason for studying—not just because it's something he "has to do". You'll also find that your child will be more inclined to work on projects for a longer time in teams than alone.

At an intro level, you'll want to help your child plan study groups that talk things out or also tend to be more focused on concrete facts than possibilities.

At a practice stage, expect to have a group that combines work and play. This group will be flexible and tolerant of changing agendas. You can also expect this group to be energized by deadlines.

Once it's time to get down to business on completing a challenging assignment, however, your child needs a quiet, distraction-free space in which to concentrate...which means it's time for the study group to disband for the night.

Your Child's Optimal Study Buddies

The wheel below shows which temperaments work best with your child at intro (seed), practice (sprout) and growth (grass) phases of learning.

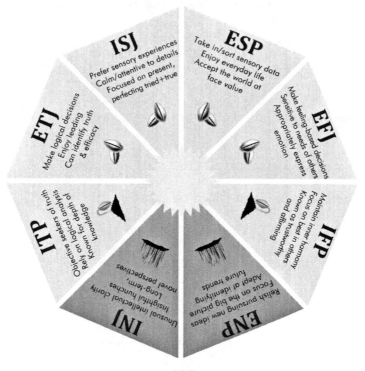

ISJ
Prefer sensory experiences
Calm/attentive to details
Focused on present,
perfecting tried+true

ESP
Take in/sort sensory data
Enjoy everyday life
Accept the world at
face value

ETJ
Make logical decisions
Enjoy leading
Can identify truth
& efficacy

EFJ
Make feeling-based decisions
Sensitive to needs of others
Appropriately express
emotion

ITP
Objective seekers of truth
Rely on logical analysis
Known for depth of
knowledge

IFP
Maintain inner harmony
Focus on best in others
Known as trustworthy
and affirming

INJ
Unusual intellectual clarity
Insightful hunches
Long-term,
novel perspectives

ENP
Relish pursuing new ideas
Focus on the big picture
Adept at identifying
future trends

Group Learning for an ETJ Child

As an extravert, your child finds group discussions and debates to be particularly effective in cementing a definitive position in subject matter. If your child's teacher is employing a technique that many teachers now use called "flipping the classroom," it's more important than usual to provide opportunities to help your child talk his way toward understanding each night...whether it be with peer study groups or with you, a sibling, or a caregiver. Otherwise, he may enter the classroom feeling unprepared for the classwork.

At an intro level, you'll want to help your child plan study groups that don't mind playing devil's advocate with each other and use logical decision making to reach closure as quickly as possible. If you are a feeling personality type, you may bristle at how this group seems to be almost harsh and judgmental with their feedback, but the reality is that they value truth over tact. For kids like your child, "giving it to them straight" is a sign of respect. Your child may, in fact, sound more stalwart in his decisions than he truly is.

By sharing how his opinions differ within a group that has come to other unique decisions along logical paths, your child will be more likely to be open to other conclusions when delving deeper into the subject with personality types who layer how decisions affect people into their conclusions.

One of the best ways to use a study group with your child is to get the students together immediately after a project is assigned to make sure that everyone is in agreement on the evaluation criteria, what interim steps need to be taken to produce an acceptable project, and to discuss how long each group member believes the individual steps will take to complete.

Your Child's Optimal Study Buddies

The wheel below shows which temperaments

work best with your child at intro (seed), practice

(sprout) and growth (grass) phases of learning.

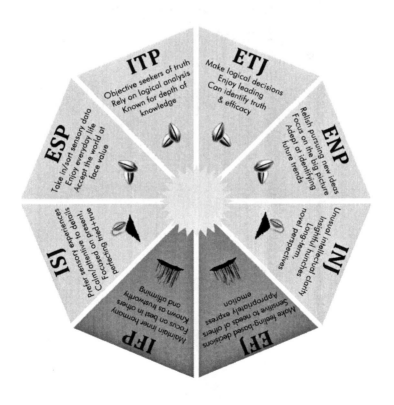

Group Learning for an IFP Child

As an introvert, your child needs a chance to fully read, reflect on and digest information before feeling comfortable engaging in a group discussion. In school, this is a technique that many teachers now use called "flipping the classroom," and is a good model for how you should approach group learning for your child.

Don't make the mistake of thinking that because your child is an introvert, he won't thrive in study groups. Introverts can work very well in teams, as long as the groups stay small or, better yet, are one-on-one.

At an intro level, you'll want to help your child plan study groups that understand the human side of things. Don't expect the group to get down to business, as they take their relationships just as seriously as the assignment (if not more so). You will need to work with your child to feel comfortable giving and receiving constructive criticism, as they will be likely to agree with others in the group just for the sake of harmony and will often choose tact over truth to avoid clashes.

One of the best ways to use a study group with your child is to get the students together during each project phase to be cheerleaders for each other, as their belief in each other can improve a feeling group's performance across the board. This said, in long-term assignments, it's absolutely vital for your child to include a broader range of personality types, since he will need both a "hater" and a motivator in order to complete a truly polished final product...even if the conflict is initially upsetting.

Your Child's Optimal Study Buddies

The wheel below shows which temperaments work best with your child at intro (seed), practice (sprout) and growth (grass) phases of learning.

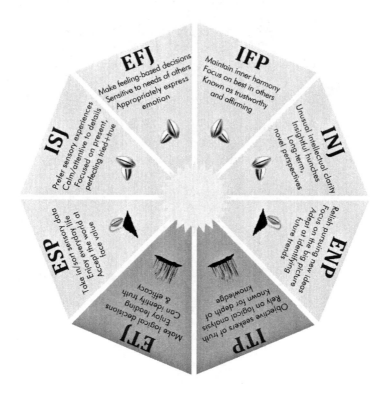

Group Learning for an INJ Child

As an introvert, your child needs to have a chance to fully read, reflect and digest information before feeling comfortable engaging in a group discussion. In school, this is a technique that many teachers now use called "flipping the classroom," which is a good model for how you should approach group learning for your child.

Don't make the mistake of thinking that because your child is an introvert, he won't thrive in study groups. Introverts can work very well in teams, as long as the groups stay small.

At an intro level, you'll want to help your child plan study groups that think things through before offering perspectives, or that tend to look for abstract patterns and meaning beneath the surface of things rather than initially shaping understanding based on facts and details.

At a practice stage, expect to have a group that likes to stick to an organized agenda and focus on work before breaking for play. This group will feel anxious with a looming deadline, so they will most likely get down to business quickly to allow ample time to systematically study and practice.

One of the best ways to use a study group with your child is to get the students together to review late-stage drafts of challenging assignments, as this final opportunity for discussion can improve the group's performance across the board.

YOUR CHILD'S OPTIMAL STUDY BUDDIES

The wheel below shows which temperaments

work best with your child at intro (seed), practice

(sprout) and growth (grass) phases of learning.

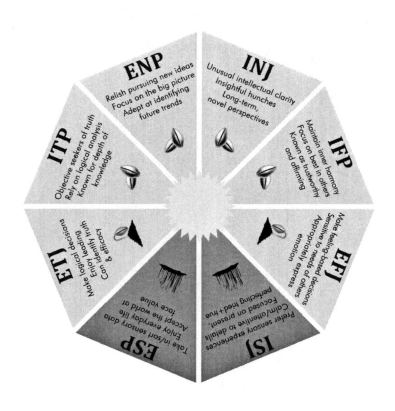

Group Learning for an ISJ Child

As an introvert, your child needs to have a chance to fully read, reflect and digest information before feeling comfortable engaging in a group discussion. In school, this is a technique that many teachers now use called "flipping the classroom," which is a good model for how you should approach group learning for your child.

Don't make the mistake of thinking that because your child is an introvert, he won't thrive in study groups. Introverts can work very well in teams, as long as the groups stay small.

At an intro level, you'll want to help your child plan study groups that think things through before offering perspectives, or that tend to be more focused on concrete facts than possibilities.

At a practice stage, expect to have a group that likes to stick to an organized agenda and will focus on work before breaking for play. This group will feel anxious with a looming deadline, so they will most likely get down to business quickly to allow ample time to systematically study and practice.

One of the best ways to use a study group with your child is to get the students together to review late-stage drafts of challenging assignments, as this final opportunity for discussion can improve the group's performance across the board.

Your Child's Optimal Study Buddies

The wheel below shows which temperaments
work best with your child at intro (seed), practice
(sprout) and growth (grass) phases of learning.

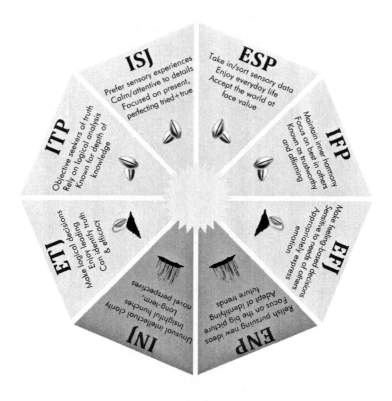

The wheel contains the following temperament descriptions:

ISJ — Prefer sensory experiences, Calm/attentive to details, Focused on present, perfecting tried+true

ESP — Take in/sort sensory data, Enjoy everyday life, Accept the world at face value

ITP — Objective seekers of truth, Rely on logical analysis, Known for depth of knowledge

IFP — Maintain inner harmony, Focus on best in others, Known as trustworthy and affirming

ETJ — Make logical decisions, Enjoy leading truth, Can identify truth & efficacy

EFJ — Make feeling-based decisions, Sensitive to needs of others, Appropriately express emotion

INJ — Unusual intellectual clarity, Insightful hunches, Long-term, novel perspectives

ENP — Relish pursuing new ideas, Focus on the big picture, Adept at identifying future trends

Group Learning for an ITP Child

As an introvert, your child needs a chance to fully read, reflect on and digest information before feeling comfortable engaging in a group discussion. In school, this is a technique that many teachers now use called "flipping the classroom," and is a good model for how you should approach group learning for your child.

Don't make the mistake of thinking that because your child is an introvert, he won't thrive in study groups. Introverts can work very well in teams, as long as the groups stay small or, better yet, are one-on-one.

At an intro level, you'll want to help your child plan study groups that don't mind playing devil's advocate with each other to fully understand the potential cause-and-effect branches. If you have a feeling personality type, you may bristle at how this group seems to cut to the core with their feedback and value truth over tact. For kids like your child, "giving it to them straight" is a sign of respect. This said, if the group disagrees, they may be surprised that their conclusions are not universally shared. However, by sharing how his opinions differ within a group that has come to other unique decisions along logical paths, your child will be more likely to be open to other conclusions when delving deeper into the subject with personality types that layer how decisions affect people into their conclusions.

One of the best ways to use a study group with your child is to get the students together during each project phase to be critics for each other, as the group can appreciate debating and questioning the pros and cons of each perspective and will help each other clarify evaluation criteria set by the teacher. This said, in long-term assignments, it's absolutely vital for your child to include a broader range of personality types, since he will need to layer in the human element in order to fully flesh out his understanding.

Your Child's Optimal Study Buddies

The wheel below shows which temperaments

work best with your child at intro (seed), practice

(sprout) and growth (grass) phases of learning.

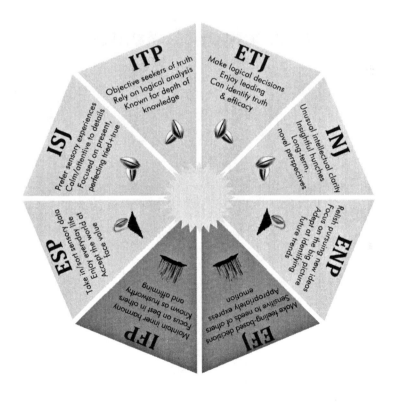

Enrichment Activities

"It's what we're excited about that educates us."

~Lives on the Boundary.

Rose, M. (1995)

A mother raven flew over a swan swimming in a lake, and thought him unspeakably beautiful. Believing that his fine white color came from washing in the water in which he swam, the raven left her nest and took her chicks to live near the lake. But no matter how often she washed her baby birds' feathers in the water, their black color never changed. Instead the birds all nearly starved because the food they ate did not exist near the lake. Once the mother raven realized the error of her ways, the family of birds returned to their native home and flourished because they were able to nourish themselves as nature intended.

When we as parents attempt to transform our children into different kinds of kids—what we wish they would be, think they should be, or key into what they *can* do versus what they *prefer* to do—we deny their spirits nourishment.

While we may have to live with one-size-fits-all

during the school day, we have an opportunity to feed their spirits with extracurricular activities, and celebrate who they were born to be.

As parents, we want to give our kids the chance to discover inner strengths that can turn into adult careers that they are truly excited about—not just logging 40 hours a week to pay the bills. One of the best ways for parents to accomplish this goal is via enrichment activities. Unfortunately, today's parents are all too familiar with scenarios where a child begs to enroll in a certain extracurricular activity, only to decide two weeks into the session that he can't stand it. So, the parents are left to either (a) write off the money spent on the series of classes or (b) drag the child kicking and screaming to the remaining lessons week after week as his initial interest in the subject dwindles.

This chapter will reveal how to avoid these scenarios and instead stimulate your child's appetite for learning.

Regardless, however, of your child's personality type, here are some key questions to ask to ensure that the program, teacher and curriculum are a good match for *your* standards as a parent.

☐ What is the teacher-to-student ratio in your available classes?

☐ What is your philosophy with regard to discipline?

☐ What is your drop-in policy?

☐ How will you communicate with me with regard to program happenings (e.g., games, recitals, holidays, etc.)

☐ How long have you taught at this particular location?

☐ What is the turnover rate of the rest of the staff?

☐ Is the program licensed by an applicable state agency?

☐ Check that the lessons will be taught in a safe and healthy space. (Are the materials clean? Are first-aid kits available? Do any outdoor play spaces have fences or natural boundaries?)

☐ Check the Megan's Law database for the name/address of the potential instructor.

☐ Don't forget to ask for a few recent parent references.

The Extraverted Feeling Child's Ideal Enrichment Activity Theme

ACTIVE COOPERATION

Team Sports; Student Government; Theater/ Dance/Music Productions; Volunteerism; Cultural Activities; Animal Care; Scouting; Journalism.

If you are able to provide unstructured time as well as structured opportunities for areas of passion, you'll be giving your child the opportunity to develop his private speech—the ability to better understand his own emotions and behavior—which can sometimes be neglected by extraverted feelers because of their desire to please others. This self-directed learning will also give your child the opportunity to further explore and practice his natural gift for sensitivity and an emotional, harmonious, values-based understanding the world.

If you have a chance to meet the teacher or—better yet—
see the classroom, beforehand, you should definitely
seize the opportunity with your child. This "preview"
can be incredibly beneficial for him, as it ensures that
he makes a personal connection with the teacher.

What To Look For...

...IN ACTIVITIES:

- Group activities

- Activities that encourage your child's
  natural curiosity about different
  cultures, religions or viewpoints

- Sports teams that friends will also be on

- Active, physical camps and activities

- As a natural nurturer, your child would do well in a
  camp or activity where he is on the older end of the
  age range and can help care for the younger students

- Be sure to schedule time for you and your child
  to do something special together "just the two
  of you," and as a family on a regular basis

...IN TEACHERS:

- Warm coaches who play "for the fun of it"

- Teachers who accept and acknowledge feelings as valid, and are tolerant of a bit of rambling

What to Avoid...

...In Activities:

- Sedentary, quiet camps or activities

- Because of your child's natural bent toward sticking to a game plan, select activities in which he can feel at ease in the predictability of a daily routine, and know the rules of the activities you choose

- Mean or negative students in class

- Classes where conflict or critique is a part of the agenda—for instance, debate

...IN TEACHERS:

- Unemotional teachers and coaches who encourage your child to "snap out of it" or "toughen up" after an emotional outburst

- Teachers who yell or have a tendency to reprimand harshly

- Competitive coaches who will do whatever it takes to win

The Extraverted Intuitive

Child's Ideal Enrichment Activity Theme

DABBLING AND PERFORMING

Art Classes; Performing Arts (e.g. Music, Dance or Theater; Outdoor Activities/Games; Team Sports; Design/Invention/Creative Opportunities; Debate; Daring Sports like BMX, Surfing or Skateboarding.

Extraverted intuitive kids like your child have a natural tendency to overextend themselves or "flake" on commitments—so it's important to help him hone decision-making skills in this regard by working through pros and cons of the often dizzying array of options together.

Because kids like your child adore starting projects, but have a hard time finishing them, it's important to reinforce following through on the full commitment to the activity or series of lessons.

It's also very important to help your child understand what it takes to master a skill. So, even if he dabbles in a variety of different activities, be sure to pick one activity in which to work toward mastery. It can be eye opening to talk about Malcolm Gladwell's finding (in *Outliers*) that it takes 10,000 hours of effort to become an expert at anything. Talking about how many hours this is in the context of musical instrument lessons or sports practice can give your child a more concrete impression of the path ahead, so that you can decide together the activity in which he is willing to put forth extraordinary, focused effort.

What To Look For...

...IN ACTIVITIES:

- A variety of activities and new experiences

- Improvisational theater is a favorite of your child's personality type, as is anything with humor and fantasy

- Open-ended day camps where there's something new to learn or do each day

- Group activities—particularly ones where your child has an opportunity to lead

- Activities that capitalize on your child's passion for design and invention

- Team sports

- Opportunities for an "audience," particularly those where your child can be the center of attention

...IN TEACHERS:

- Teachers who allow your child to think out loud

- Teachers who enforce meaningful rules are in a better position to rein in your child's innate desire to bend the rules

- Teachers who are tolerant of "why" questions and give direct, clear answers— even if that answer is, "I'm not sure"

What to Avoid...

...IN ACTIVITIES:

- Quiet, sedentary classes that thrive on order

- Lots of alone time

...IN TEACHERS:

- Teachers who are intolerant of or don't know how to effectively deal with your child's boundary-pushing nature

- Teachers more focused on the details than the big picture

- Teachers who have "a certain way of doing things" instead of going with the flow of the current class

The Extraverted Sensing Child's Ideal Enrichment Activity Theme

VARIED NEW ADVENTURES

Hands-On Science Classes; Community Theater; Day Camps; Dance Classes; Outdoor/Nature-based Activities; Gardening; Baking Classes; Team Sports; Adventurous Activities (e.g., Surfing, SCUBA, BMX, Skateboarding); "Trendy" Classes; Cheerleading; Arts & Crafts; Community Cause-Based Activities (e.g., "going green"; Helping in a Soup Kitchen; Walk-a-Thons).

Today's trend toward experiential education is tailor-made for extraverted sensing kids. Words just don't take on the same meaning or importance as actions to kids like your child. (You've probably experienced this at home when telling your child not to do something countless times doesn't have nearly the impact of his actually experiencing the cause and effect of his actions.) So, be sure to look for classes that allow your child to be an active, involved participant as much as possible during the activities.

Because extraverted sensors like your child take the world at face value, it's also very important to help your child cement school friendships in enrichment activities with kind, caring and genuine kids who can help you reinforce that it's what's INSIDE that counts.

What To Look For...

...IN ACTIVITIES:

- Activities where your child is taught how to safely "get his pulse racing"

- Lots of variation

- Activities that require speed or dexterity

- Reality-based classes

- Learning structured as games

- Day or week-long activities vs. month or summer-long activities

- Surprise or spontaneous activities or family days

- Outdoor activities

...IN TEACHERS:

- Energetic teachers

- Spontaneous teachers

- Consistent class rules and limits

- Swift and predictable discipline

- Teachers that practice positive reinforcement

What to Avoid...

...IN ACTIVITIES:

- Sedentary or quiet classes

- Open-ended time alone where your child becomes bored

- Classes that are too abstract

...IN TEACHERS:

- Teachers who could be perceived as playing favorites

- Vague expectations of behavior

- Teachers more focused on the big picture than the details

The Extraverted Thinking Child's Ideal Enrichment Activity Theme

ACCOLADES & LEADERSHIP

Debate Classes; Theater "Direction"; Scripted Theater or Music; School Government; Volunteering; Scouting; Competitive Team and Individual Sports.

Make sure you and your child both "interview" the coach or teacher prior to enrolling him in the class, as your child finds it more challenging than most other personality types to tolerate incompetence—even if it's just a case of perception versus reality. Work together to create a full list of options, then weigh the pros and cons of all of them before making a few top choices. While your child will do his best to excel in all of them, his high standard of excellence for himself may be exhausting. It also provides many potential points of failure to work around when things don't go exactly as planned.

What To Look For...

...IN ACTIVITIES:

- Activities where your child is on the young end of the age range

- Classes that have a structure, agenda or game plan

- Activities in which your child has an opportunity to take a leadership role

- Activities where your child can be appreciated and applauded for both his abilities and competence

- Activities where participants have the opportunity to win trophies, awards or ribbons at the end

- Classes that afford the satisfaction of finishing projects

...IN TEACHERS:

- Teachers who value truth over tact when it comes to critique

- Teachers who are perceived as fair and consistent

- Teachers who will admit "I don't know" if they don't know the answer, yet encourage your child's probing nature

- Teachers who encourage mutual respect

between themselves and students

- Coaches who strive to win or be the best

- Teachers who value student perspectives

What to Avoid...

...In Activities:

- Open-ended classes that move in the directions that "the wind takes them"

- Improvisational acting

- Classes without predetermined criteria for evaluation

- Quiet and sedentary classes

...IN TEACHERS:

- Teachers who communicate from an emotional tact instead of a logical one

- "Touchy-feely" teachers

- Teachers who don't follow a routine or agenda

- Coaches who play "for the fun of it" instead of to win

The Introverted Feeling Child's Ideal Enrichment Activity Theme

CREATIVITY & MEANING

Music; Reading; Creative Writing Classes; Open-ended Art Classes like Drawing, Painting or Clay; Figure Skating; Theater; Dance; Religious/Belief-Based Classes; Volunteer Opportunities that have "Meaning"; Horseback Riding; Animal Care

If you are able to provide unstructured time for these personal types of pursuits, you'll be giving your child the opportunity to develop his private speech—the ability to control his own emotions and behavior. This private speech (also known as executive function) is used by adults countless times as we work to innovate and invent. This self-directed learning will also give your child the opportunity to further explore and practice his natural gift for sensitivity and an emotional, harmonious, values-based understanding the world.

If you have a chance to meet the teacher or—better yet— see the classroom, beforehand, you should definitely seize the opportunity with your child. This "preview" can be incredibly beneficial for him, as it helps ensure that he makes a personal connection with the teacher.

What To Look For...

...IN ACTIVITIES:

- Classes with gentle and creative students in the class mix

- Classes that allow your child to express himself

- Cooperative, loosely structured classroom environments

- Unstructured fitness activities (For instance, shooting hoops, dancing to the radio, bike riding, hiking)

- Opportunities to expand your child's collections of objects that are meaningful to him

- Small group or one-on-one classroom environments

...IN TEACHERS:

- Teachers who are understanding, reassuring and loving

- Teachers who are patient and tolerant of emotions

- Teachers with similar personalities who have learned how to stay organized and set/meet goals

- Teachers who can communicate very specific expectations and give your child ample praise

What to Avoid...

...In Activities:

- Large group activities

- Activities/games where rules are never bent, even in extenuating circumstances

- Overscheduling activities and limiting free time

- Competitive games or sports

- Activities which require your child to be the center of attention for any length of time (rather than leaving the option open to the student)

- Mean or negative students in class

...IN TEACHERS:

- Overly critical teachers, as kids like your child get their feelings hurt easily

- Unemotional teachers and coaches that encourage your child to "snap out of it" or "toughen up" after an emotional outburst

- Very structured teachers who are intolerant of daydreaming

- Teachers who like "tidy" classes

- Teachers who yell or have a tendency to reprimand harshly

The Introverted Intuitive Child's Ideal Enrichment Activity Theme

Intellectual Exploration

Writing; Composing; Choreography; Abstract Art Classes; Invention-Oriented Science Classes; Anything Theory-Based; Classes Perceived as "Cutting Edge"; Discovery-Oriented Classes

Kids with personalities like your child's relish an abundance of free time to "deep dive" into the subjects that most interest and inspire them.

As a parent, remember that this free time actually helps kids develop their "private speech"—the ability to control their own emotions and behavior. Private speech (also known as executive function)

is used by adults countless times as we work to innovate and invent. Instead of over-scheduling your child, provide him with free time for independent exploration and squash any fearful feelings on your part of "what hasn't he learned yet" with a more joyful "what will he think of next?" Given the opportunity, chances are good that your child will delight you.

In the same vein, spend the money you would have spent on additional activities to provide your child with the supplies and equipment he needs to further investigate and explore his theories and passions.

What To Look For...

...IN ACTIVITIES:

- Often, the most appealing musical instruments are those that have an ethereal quality, such as the flute or harp

- If you select a group activity for your child, make sure it's a small group with at least a couple of kids he knows

- Classes that will help you celebrate your child's passion for pioneering and new ideas

- Classes that allow your child to play "detective" and solve mysteries

- Because your child's personality lends itself to intellectual development more than athletic development, it's best to select physical activities that are either one-on-one or small groups where your child is on the older end of the spectrum

...IN TEACHERS:

- Teachers who will allow your child to finish creative projects before showing them off

- Teachers who encourage your child's exploring nature and desire to "dig deeper"

- Teachers who give your child a chance to use imagination and creativity to think outside the box

What to Avoid...

...IN ACTIVITIES:

- Sudden changes in activities or schedules

- Activities that require a lot of interaction or socialization with lots of new people

- Classes where your child will be put in a position where he is required to be the center of attention

- Overscheduling, as introverted intuitive kids relish privacy and alone time to daydream

...IN TEACHERS:

- Teachers who expect compliance without question

- Teachers who expect students to follow a specific, preset "way of doing things"

- Teachers who focus on facts or specifics versus the big idea

The Introverted Sensing Child's Ideal Enrichment Activity Theme

FAMILIARITY & FINE MOTOR SKILLS

Scrapbooking; Sewing; Jewelry Making; Cooking
Classes; Legos; Music; Knitting; Model Building;
Mosaic/Decoupage Art; Nature Classes; Animal Care;
Stamp or Coin Collecting; Scouting; Arts Appreciation;
Team or Individual Sports; "How-To" Classes

If you are able to provide unstructured time for
these types of sensory rich activities, you'll be giving
your child the opportunity to develop their private
speech—the ability to control his own emotions
and behavior. This private speech (also known as
executive function) is used by adults countless times
as we work to innovate and invent. This self-directed
learning will also give your child the opportunity

to pace his natural gift for understanding the world as we see, smell, touch, taste and hear it.

If you have a chance to meet the teacher or—better yet—see the classroom beforehand, you should definitely seize the opportunity with your child. This "preview" can be incredibly beneficial for your child in order to make sure he feels as comfortable and confident as possible on the first day.

What To Look For...

...IN ACTIVITIES:

- Activities that are aligned with your child's gender (e.g., ballet for girls, football for boys)

- One-on-one and small classes that one or more close friends will also be attending

- Classes with an end goal, result or work product in mind

- Classes in which your child can feel he has done something correctly.

- "Appreciation" classes where your child can dissect what makes something great (e.g., art, film, music, literature)

...IN TEACHERS:

- Teachers that adhere to strict schedules and like order and rules, as well as routine

- Familiar environments and teachers

- Teachers that clearly communicate what is expected of the students via clear direction and guidance (e.g., step-by-step approaches)

- Teachers that allow your child time to acclimate to the new setting

What to Avoid...

...IN ACTIVITIES:

- Large group classes

- A variety of activities and teachers

- "Adventurous" activities

- Activities in which your child is the center of attention for any length of time

...IN TEACHERS:

- Overly emotional or overbearing teachers

- Teachers that focus more on ideas than facts

- "Spontaneous" teachers with vague or open daily agendas

The Introverted Thinking Child's Ideal Enrichment Activity Theme

PROBLEM-SOLVING AND STRATEGY

Technology/Computing Classes; Video Game Development; Individual Sports; Strategy Clubs (e.g. chess or bridge); Building Classes (e.g. LEGOs, model trains); Model Making; Experimental Science Classes; Nature Walks/Hikes; "Inventing" Workshops

If you are able to provide unstructured time for these personal types of pursuits, you'll be giving your child the opportunity to develop his private speech—the ability to control his own emotions and behavior. This private speech (also known as executive function) is used by adults countless times as we work to innovate and invent. This self-directed learning will also give your

child the opportunity to further explore and practice
his natural gift for figuring things out in his own way
and to analyze before reacting on his own timetable.
Finally, unstructured opportunities for learning provide
introverted thinkers like your child with opportunities
to try a new skill without concern about appearing
incompetent. (Introverted thinkers fear their own
incompetence more than most other personality types.)

Be sure to talk about the teacher's credentials with your
child prior to the first class. A belief that his new teacher
is a competent subject area expert will ensure that
your child listens to opinions that may differ from his
own. It's also critical to alert the teacher to your child's
questioning nature and insure that he understands
the importance of providing specific critiques for
improvement as opposed to general feedback like
"great job!" or "that wasn't what I was looking for."

What To Look For...

...IN ACTIVITIES:

- Activities that allow your child to dig into "how things work"

- Classes that allow your child to explore and problem-solve

- An innate specialist, let your child guide you into the activities he is most interested in—even if it means several activities that sound remarkably similar

- Classes with a steep learning curve

- Passion-based classes where your child is at the younger end of the age spectrum

- Classes that allow for hypothesis, objective analysis and logical

- Competitive activities

- More and more advanced classes that move your child in the direction of becoming a master of the subject area

...IN TEACHERS:

- Teachers that value truth over tact when it comes to critique

- Teachers that are perceived as fair and consistent

- One-on-one teaching environments with clearly defined expectations

- Teachers that place high value on

uniqueness and creative thinking

- Teachers that your child respects (generally considered an expert in his or her field)

What to Avoid...

...IN ACTIVITIES:

- Large group activities

- Activities/games where rules are occasionally bent

- Activities in which your child is required to be at the center of attention for any length of time (e.g., goalie on a team, piano recital)

- Overly emotional students in class

- Repetitive or routine classes or camps

...IN TEACHERS:

- Emotional teachers

- Teachers or coaches that can be perceived as "unfair" (e.g. the parent of another child in the class)

- Teachers that value punctuality, structured schedules and order

- Teachers that require or encourage vocal class participation

- Teachers that are intolerant of or frustrated by your child's absentmindedness

Motivation and Underachievement

"The best coaches know how to read the motivation patterns of their players. Whether the knack came to them intuitively or with much intentional study, they know what to do."

~*Finding the Zone.*

Lawrence, G. (2010)

A *hungry fox noticed a delicious looking bunch of grapes growing beyond mouth's reach high on a vine. He leaped and jumped from the ground several times as he snapped at the vine. Sadly, try as he might, he could not reach a single juicy grape.*

Disappointed by his fruitless efforts, he stopped trying and instead said, with a shrug, to comfort himself, "Oh, they were probably sour anyway!"

His mother looked on from far away, dismayed, because she saw that if he had thought a little longer or tried a little harder, he could not only have achieved his goal, but gained confidence that he could achieve the seemingly impossible when obstacles presented themselves in the future.

Underachievement is one of the most challenging, frustrating experiences for a parent because you know in your heart, mind or *both* that your child is capable of more...but just isn't putting forth the necessary effort to achieve what's being asked of them.

The different personality types exhibit underachievement in different ways. And, just as you've seen in the other chapters of this book, the way you underachieve may not be the same way that your child underachieves. As a result, you may not always be on the lookout for his early signs of underachievement so that you can both nip them in the bud and key into the best ways to motivate your child.

Even if you never need to return to this particular chapter in the future due to underachievement, you'll have at your fingertips the best ways to motivate your child in ways that will resonate with him.

Motivation & Underachievement for the Extraverted Feeling Child

Your Child's Most Likely Underachievement Profile ::

Social Director

As we've talked about throughout this book, extraverted feelers like your child avoid disharmony like the plague and, normally, would rather echo a perspective that he doesn't necessarily believe than risk stirring the pot with a debatable opinion. Because of this preoccupation with how others feel, and socially appropriate reactions and interactions, your child will most likely work very hard to earn the validation and acceptance of his parents, teachers and peers. The mass media provides the structure and guidelines for what's culturally and socially acceptable, so most likely your child already looks the part. The challenge comes in as a result of your child's natural desire to do what everyone else wants him to do,

which can mean biting off more than he can chew.

If either parents or teachers devalue other kids in class

or put down their opinions, the problem can escalate.

Your child may become angry with the person(s)

he feels should be looking out for him for not doing

their job, and will shift his focus from trying to please

authority figures to prioritizing popularity instead.

Motivating Your Child

- Help your child understand that he can't take care of everything for everybody, and refocus him on what's necessary to accomplish right now for himself, in order to help more people in the long run.

- If a teacher relationship is not strong, keep your child focused on how his understanding of the content or subject can benefit others... either in the short- or long-term.

- Encourage study groups—particularly in classes where he doesn't connect well with the teacher— to help each other come to a consensus on their understanding of the material, and talk through decisions together. If a group does not seem to work well together, try shifting out some of the participants. (For your child, how the group works together is equally or even more important than what is ultimately accomplished.)

- Ask your child to tell you how he feels about each class or teacher on a regular basis. If he opens up about a subject in which he is struggling, listen and share techniques you used to overcome them—or, better yet, invite a family member with a more similar personality to share strategies that they used successfully in a similar situation. Create a plan of attack together. These self-disclosures not only bond you more closely, but will help your child feel appreciated and understood, and play to his innate desire to build consensus with respect to decisions and game plans.

- Be a cheerleader during times of both struggle and success, as your child responds more strongly than other personality types to positive reinforcement.

- Reward behavior, effort, and attitude instead of result.

Motivation & Underachievement for the Extraverted Intuitive Child

Your Child's Most Likely Underachievement Profile ::

Living on the Edge

As we've talked about throughout this book, extraverted intuitives like your child perform best under the pressure of a deadline. In fact, your child is often thinking about the solution or assignment long before putting pen to paper. (Something that can be tough for judging-type parents to understand.)

However, when not reined in, your child's desire for newness combined with his broad strokes mentality and boundary-pushing nature, can result in incomplete or poorly executed work.

Your child will often help others excel on a project

that he himself doesn't complete. Your child may even seem to purposely avoid sustained success simply because he doesn't put in the time to get it right.

The more you or the teacher focus on your child, however, the more likely he is to learn to keep sabotaging himself. Your child may start off with the best of intentions, but give up if he can't quickly figure out how to get from here to there or if he has gotten off-track.

When he is doing things right, he is left to his own devices to figure out the next step. When your child does things wrong, someone pays attention to him and helps him get to the right answer or fill in the missing pieces more rapidly than if he had completed the assignment himself.

Motivating Your Child

- Maintain steady availability in times of both failure and success

- Focus on future goals and how this work is a stepping stone to achieving those goals

- Help plan out a success strategy in the beginning so that your child has your guidance during the planning process, then let him loose

- Encourage your child to find new or original ways to accomplish seemingly routine homework tasks

- Engage your child's natural curiosity and interest in possibilities and the "butterfly effect" of concept understanding

- Find the "newness" in topics

- Find mentors who are willing to be conceptual "tour guides" and help your child imagine where this new knowledge could lead

- Be willing to be a sounding board for stream-of-consciousness conversations or brainstorms about challenges your child may be having in school...or even just projects

- If your child seems to be frustrated by the details, help him shift focus to the bigger picture for a while before refocusing on the particulars

Motivation & Underachievement for the Extraverted Sensing Child

Your Child's Most Likely Underachievement Profile ::

Good Time Guy

As we've talked about throughout this book, extraverted sensors like your child perform best under the pressure of a deadline. And, in most cases, your child is often thinking about an assignment long before putting pen to paper. (Something that can be tough for judging-type parents to understand.)

However, when not reined in, your child's aversion to closure combined with his passion for things he can see, smell, touch, taste or hear in the here and now (instead of write on paper) can result in incomplete or poorly executed work.

Extraverted sensors like your child like to live in the moment, and will often sacrifice future grades for fun right now...especially if he is in at the center of it. Your child's need to be the center of attention can also lead him toward creating drama to gain the attention of others. Studying and homework play second fiddle to what's going on with friends. However, his peer relationships are often shaded by competition and friendships are more "alliances" than reflective of emotional intimacy.

Your child's pull toward the concrete and tangible leads to his perception of material goods and having things done for him as love. So, incentives like toys or movies for good grades may work in the short term, but will eventually make this pattern worse instead of better as no incentive will come to mean "not important" to your child.

Motivating Your Child

- Your child draws his self-worth from how many people notice and admire him and his self-perception is a mirror of how he believes others see him, so focus on how impressive good grades are to others.

- Help your child face the facts of how his underachievement is negatively impacting his life in the here and now.

- If your child seems to be lost or overwhelmed by an assignment, help your child reveal the path of least resistance toward successful completion by breaking down the assignment into bite-sized chunks.

- Connect what your child is learning about to daily life or past challenges that would have been easier to tackle had he known about the topic in question.

- For your child more than other personality types, actions speak louder than words, so be sure to set unambiguous boundaries with actionable punishments for going out-of-bounds, and stick to them.

Motivation & Underachievement for the Extraverted Thinking Child

Your Child's Most Likely Underachievement Profile ::

Master Manipulator

Your child's potential problem behaviors are most likely to be a result of his ability to achieve a desired payoff...though the payoff not be the one desired by you or his teachers! For underachieving extraverted thinkers, their own gratification takes precedence over the desires of others and they will find a way to systematically get what they want. One technique extraverted thinkers like your child often use is the "silent treatment" to wear down authority figures to the point of giving into their demands. It's not so much disrespect for authority as an enjoyment of discovering ways to bargain their way out of commitments without consequence. It's finding the path to fulfillment of desires without greater responsibility. These kids tend to distance themselves from "human drama" and often interpret intimacy or compassion as masks for ulterior motives. Fantasies of power and success that aren't rooted in any past accomplishments or talents, but instead in their ability to exploit compassion or love as weaknesses, rather than values to emulate. One example is an extraverted thinker getting chores "wrong" in order to avoid future responsibility. Personal relationships are viewed as a chess game to attain the power/controlling position in the relationship.

If you run into this profile with your child, be sure to work with his teachers to lay out systematic, consistent consequences for underachieving, while simultaneously trying to reveal an intrinsic motivation for success that's more compelling than having someone else do his work. Clarify what your child most wants to accomplish and plan out how he can

achieve the goal in an authentic way. Emphasize that

while manipulating others to do his work may work

in the short-term, but his long-term goals cannot be

accomplished without putting forth his own effort.

Motivating Your Child

- Be assertive and consistent. Agree on discipline with his teacher so that he can rely on consistent expectations and application of rules both at home and in the classroom. (Be sure to apply any rules you have for your child to his siblings as well, as he will appreciate equality in your family by-laws!)

- Talk through the logical cause-and-effect consequences of "delegating work" before it happens, and the points of impact. (For instance, getting someone else to do the work for him will not affect the *teacher* in the future, but could negatively affect your *child's* long-term ambitions or comprehension in future classes.)

- If your child feels he already knows what he needs to without doing "busywork," clarify and reinforce the short- and long-term cause-and-effect of his choices. Try to reveal any inconsistencies or illogic in his actions.

Motivation & Underachievement for the Introverted Feeling Child

YOUR CHILD'S UNDERACHIEVEMENT PROFILE :: AVOIDANCE

As we've discussed throughout this book, introverted feelers like your child avoid disharmony like the plague and would rather not offer a perspective at all than offer one that is not in alignment with his inner values. Your child is preoccupied with how others feel about him, and feels anxious about his negative perceptions of authority figures and peers alike, so he won't react well if teachers use the "stick" approach to motivation more than a carrot. In that event,he will be more likely to not participate in, or worse yet, skip class to avoid potential conflict.

Your child prefers to engage in tasks in which he feels he is assured of success and positive feedback more than most personality types. So, while your child will make his highest grades in classes in which he feels his instructor genuinely likes him, he may struggle in classes where interactions are not as amicable. These challenges, along with your child's near-phobia of disappointing parents at home, can often result in your not knowing about his struggles or failings until it's too late to make the changes necessary to achieve a good grade.

Motivating Your Child

- Don't overprotect your child from anxiety or frustrations, but instead help him work through those emotions.

- If a teacher relationship is not strong, keep your child focused on how his understanding of the content or subject can benefit him or others...either in the short- or long-term.

- Encourage one-on-one study groups—particularly in classes in which he doesn't connect well with the teacher—to help each other better understand the material, ask questions in a "safe" space and motivate each other.

- Encourage your child to tell you how he feels about each class on a regular basis and don't discount his emotions. If he opens up about a subject in which he is struggling, talk to him about a school struggle you had in the past, but don't share the techniques you used to overcome them unless your child explicitly asks you how. These self-disclosures not only bond you more closely, but help alleviate any concerns that your child may have about your expectations.

- Be a cheerleader during times of both struggle and success, so that your child isn't afraid to talk about potentially unpleasant topics.

- Reward behavior, effort, and attitude instead of result.

Motivation & Underachievement for the Introverted Intuitive Child

YOUR CHILD'S UNDERACHIEVEMENT PROFILE :: QUESTION AUTHORITY

As we've talked about throughout this book, introverted intuitives like your child may often challenge authority and rules. And, if teachers focus on process, routine or rules, your child may rebel. In fact, introverted intuitives are often the kids with very high marks in some classes...and very low marks in others.

When not reined in, your child's preoccupation with patterns and meaning can leave him feeling that rote assignments are a waste of his mental energy. When combined with your child's stubborn nature, a power struggle can ensue and he will rush through assignments he deems "busy work," often not demonstrating the work or thought process necessary for a passing mark.

Oddly enough, your child's big-picture thinking can result in marginal marks in elementary school when answers are more frequently black and white, but he may start to blossom later, when higher-order thinking skills require transitioning into "shades of gray" in the realm of ideas, and he is called upon to weigh many conflicting opinions.

Low test scores after big-picture concept discussions at home can be indicative of the introverted intuitive's underachieving profile. In an effort to understand the general meaning of the topic, or to grasp how the topic fits into the grand scheme of things, your child may have altogether missed the details necessary to correctly answer multiple-choice test questions. What makes this underachieving profile most frustrating for parents is that your child obviously gets the gist of the class, but isn't putting forth the effort required to memorize the details and recall them for the exam.

Motivating Your Child

- When a project or homework assignment comes in, help your child understand why it's important, in the grand scheme of things, to do a good job—for example, to get into the more advanced middle or high school "track," because that's where the focus is on theory and possibilities.

- Encourage your child to brainstorm assignment ideas early, then check with the teacher to make sure the general idea is acceptable. This creative approach will make your child feel less limited and constrained, often at the root of his stubbornness.

- If your child is missing details that are required for the assignment, it's most likely because he is ignoring conflicting viewpoints that don't mesh with his theories. Do your best to help your child parallel alternate perspectives with other meaningful patterns or trends.

- If your child is struggling with a particular teacher, do your best to keep him focused on the big picture—how a low grade or test score hurts him much more than it hurts the teacher.

- If your child doesn't want to study for an exam because he feels he already gets it, make a bargain that you'll give him a pop quiz. If he gets 90% of the answers right, he doesn't need to study anymore. Then, drill into the details and make sure he understands both the forest and the trees.

- Reward behavior, effort, and attitude instead of result.

- Recognize positive patterns that have been shown to lead to success for your child and encourage him to replicate or find ways to improve a pattern that works even better.

Motivation & Underachievement for the Introverted Sensing Child

Your Child's Underachievement Profile :: Devil's in the Details

As we've talked about throughout this book, introverted sensors like your child are often obsessed with rules and minor details. And, if things don't go as planned, your child can easily get overwhelmed and become paralyzed...especially in the face of a looming deadline. (Something that can be tough for perceiving-type parents, who get energized by deadlines, to understand.)

However, when not reined in, your child's preoccupation with the details can lead to not being able to sort through what's relevant and irrelevant to the task. This place of indecision and/or not being able to bring a project to closure quickly is extremely uncomfortable for a your child's judging nature. Your child's aversion to rule-breaking will probably result in very high marks in elementary school when answers are more frequently correct or incorrect, but he may start to struggle in higher grades when higher order thinking skills require transitioning into "shades of gray" in the realm of ideas and weighing many conflicting opinions.

The more introverted sensors like your child strive for perfection, the more likely they are to "forget" homework assignments that they don't feel lived up to their perfectionist expectations. Teachers may be the first ones to identify the initial signs of underachievement for your child because he will be less vocal in class for fear of getting the wrong answer.

Low test scores after successful study sessions at home can be indicative of this underachieving profile. Layers of knowledge and opinion lead to self-doubt about test answers. This anxiety—made worse by a low resulting score—snowballs if not nipped in the

bud because, for kids like your child, the recollection of

a past event is automatically brought into the present

tense along with all the accompanying emotions.

This underachieving profile can be one of

the most heartbreaking ones for parents—

particularly in light of your child's early school

successes and drive for perfection.

Motivating Your Child

- When a project or homework assignment comes in, help your child highlight the key aspects of the task and eliminate extraneous information

- Encourage your child to create an assignment outline early on, then decide together which key facts to focus on for this particular assignment. It might also help him to get approval from his teacher on the direction he's chosen to take.

- If your child is missing insights that will be required for the assignment, it's most likely because he has chunked this knowledge with a past experience, and is ignoring conflicting viewpoints because a different version doesn't mesh with his own experience. Do your best to help your child tie in the alternate perspective with another previous experience where he was on the opposite side of the table.

- If your child is struggling with a certain subject, do your best to remember the minor details of test day—for instance, what he wore, had for breakfast, how he studied the night before, etc. If he earns a low score on the test, you can help minimize test anxiety the next time by changing these elements and making note of them. Because introverted sensors like your child replay impactful memories over and over again and experience the same emotions, anything you can do to dichotomize the past experience from the present one will psychologically help put your child in a different frame of mind in advance of the test.

- Talk to your child about prior experiences that you may have had in school and how you turned those experiences around. These self-disclosures not only bond you more closely, but help alleviate any concerns that your child may have about your expectations.

- Reward behavior, effort, and attitude instead of result.

- Recognize positive patterns that have been shown to lead to success for your child and encourage him to replicate or find ways to improve a pattern that worked even further.

Motivation & Underachievement for the Introverted Thinking Child

Your Child's Underachievement Profile :: Stubborn Student

Your child's potential problem behaviors are most likely to be a result of his natural bent toward questioning authority. If he doesn't believe the teacher to be a credible subject area expert or has heard through the grapevine that the teacher's grading practices are unfair, he is unlikely to give the teacher a fair shot from the get-go and will tune out with respect to assignments—particularly if feedback that's given on the first few homework assignments is general or subjective.

Your child will come up with every excuse in the book why the teacher's suggestions or perspectives will not work...particularly if he questions her credibility with

213

regard to the subject at hand. This logical mindset can sometimes also lead your child to rationalize inaction. There is always a logical reason why he can't get to a task when it's assigned or why it's a waste of time to complete it. More than anything else, your child resents having to do things someone else's way "just because" instead of steering his own course and would rather not do it at all than complete an illogical task.

Motivating Your Child

Tactics to overcome this underachieving profile:

- Be assertive and consistent. Follow through on discipline so that he can rely on expectations at home...even if classroom expectations and discipline are inconsistent.

- Talk through the logical cause-and-effect consequences of inaction before it happens and the points of impact. (For instance, a low grade will not affect the teacher in the future, but could negatively affect your child's long-term ambitions or future class placement.)

- If your child doesn't respect the teacher's expertise,

encourage him to find other, more renowned sources of knowledge in the domain...be they textbooks, online resources, peers or tutors.

- If your child receives general feedback from a teacher, encourage him to go in and talk to the teacher about it and find out exactly what was wrong and right with the assignment. If necessary, make it a three-way conference (parent, teacher, student) to make your child more comfortable, but remain neutral and think of yourself as a translator—not a referee.

- Use your child's natural talent for reflective observation to identify inconsistencies and irrelevancies overlooked in his reasons for not attending to the task at hand. Your child will appreciate your working with him to reflect on and understand the basic principles at work in causes or consequences of events. (For instance, a poor grade after completing an assignment too hastily.)

Handling Successes and Failures

"The principal goal of education should be creating men and women who are capable of doing NEW things, not simply repeating what other generations have done."

~Jean Piaget

A crow, nearly dying of thirst, happened upon a pitcher which had a small amount of water left in it; but when the crow put its beak into the mouth of the pitcher he found that his beak could not reach down far enough to get at it.

He tried and tried and came close to giving up in despair.

Then a thought came to him, and he took a pebble and dropped it into the pitcher. Alas, he could still not take a sip.

So he tried again with another pebble.

...and another

...and another

...and another

At last, he saw the water almost reaching his beak, and after casting in a few more pebbles he was able to quench his thirst and save his life.

Every failure brings you closer to success.

This fable illustrates the importance of the old adage, "If at first you don't succeed, try, try again." In fact, Thomas Edison's quip after 8,000 unsuccessful trials on a nickel-iron storage battery was, "Well, at least we know 8,000 things that won't work."

In an era of teaching to the test in school and avoiding mistakes at all costs, one of the most important things we need to teach our children these days is that failure in and of itself is not a negative thing. It's how we react to failure (or overcome fear of failure) that really counts.

While we've addressed more area-specific challenges in earlier chapters, this chapter will discuss larger themes with regard to perception of success and failure for your child.

Regardless of personality type, however, it's during times of struggle, frustration and failure that your child will most need to fall back on an effective

coping strategy. Take a look at your child's Kidzmet®

preference profile and try suggesting activities that

blend 2-3 of these multiple intelligences together

to take your child's mind from a place of fear, anger

or frustration into a calmer or more joyful space.

Handling Successes & Failures with an Extraverted Feeler

Nothing means more to your child than close bonds with friends, teachers and family members. As such, one of the greatest gifts you can give him is to place a high value on your emotional relationship with him.

CHALLENGE 1 :: WHAT DO YOU MEAN TAKE EMOTION OUT OF THE EQUATION?

For extraverted feelers like your child, emotion is the lens through which they prefer to interpret the world. Especially in times of struggle, it will be difficult for him to take an objective look at the assignment or problem. When he is struggling with a problem, talk through ways to fix the problem in addition to providing a shoulder to cry on. (Become the stereotypical bartender!)

Make sure you voice your appreciation of both

incremental and long-term contributions, and make your praise feeling-, people- or relationship-oriented. For instance, "You did such an amazing job of helping X accomplish Y!" or "Thank you for ____." Be ready to recall these positive outcomes in the event of test-based or assignment-based anxiety. For instance, "You got an A on your past essay with this teacher. I'm positive you can do it again!" or "When we talked to your teacher after you got the C on the last essay, she said the things you need to focus on were A, B and C. You've been working hard to focus on those things, so you and I will be proud of your effort no matter what grade you end up receiving."

CHALLENGE 2 : TAKING ON THE WEIGHT OF THE WORLD

Because of your child's need to feel needed, he may tend to take on the emotional burdens of friends and relatives. There's no other personality type that works harder to make sure everyone's voices are heard, acknowledged and respected. To your child it doesn't even seem to matter whether the people they are helping would like their help.

It's important to reinforce to your child on a regular basis that we are all human and imperfect. Whenever something comes up where another individual is apathetic or devalues the needs of one of his friends, and he takes on the cause, be sure to talk to him about how, while taking care of people is one of his special gifts, other people don't always have those insights. While it's wonderful that he stands up for the "little guy", he may not be able to solve all of his friend's problems. Sometimes, just being there for his friend has to be enough.

CHALLENGE 3 : TACT VERSUS TRUTH

While your child has a special gift for knowing exactly what to say or do to make people feel good—whether they are warm and fuzzy occasions like birthdays or tough situations like funerals—his tendency to avoid conflict can lead to sweeping problems under the carpet, giving praise while omitting criticism, or fudging the truth completely to avoid hurting someone's feelings. Your challenge as a parent will be to model effective constructive criticism and show him by example how he can use techniques to be both tactful AND truthful:

1. Show your child that he can be truthful and minimize hurt feelings by sharing your intentions before critiquing his behavior or performance.

2. Be sure to clarify your expectations before you provide any feedback, and

3. Reinforce after offering the feedback that you are judging the what he has done or how he has done it, not who he is, and that being able to trust each other to be truthful is one of the best ways of having a close relationship.

Handling Successes & Failures with an Extraverted Intuitive

You probably know first hand that making big mistakes is not a big deal for your child. In fact, extraverted intuitives like your child are more likely to feel that playing it safe is a boring and dreadful way to live, and tackle major challenges with ferocious determination. It's this willingness to fail that makes him so creative and inventive.

On the other hand, your child probably tends to sweat the small stuff and can be irritable and impatient about small setbacks or when what many would deem simply nuisances occur. If he can't get over the minor bumps, it can lead to...

CHALLENGE 1 :: PERSEVERANCE

Because of your child's natural preference for breadth

versus depth, he may tend to move on to other pursuits
instead of persevering through the challenge.

One place you may see this clearly exhibited is with
enrichment activities. An extraverted intuitive like your
child will dive headlong into a brand new enrichment
activity, making progress in leaps and bounds.
However, when he gets to the small, incremental gains
that are borne of practice, his tendency is to give
up the original passion for a shiny new one and feel
like he just "wasn't good at" the original pursuit.

For this reason, it's important to keep him focused
on the end goal instead of the next step in order to
help him see the value in perseverance. Talk with
your child about any doubts or challenges, and move
him back into the idea phase by brainstorming how
to overcome them, in order to reinvigorate him.

Instead of celebrating incremental successes, celebrate longer-term ones and talk about how far he has come and how much further he could take the pursuit.

CHALLENGE 2 : BIG DREAMS TAKE TIME

Another key potential source of perceived failure comes as a result of your child's drive to change what is into what could be...and how tough it may be to get others excited about the possibilities he sees.

As you have probably already witnessed, your child gets frustrated or annoyed with those who cannot see the big picture and has a hard time with "closed-minded" people. This is because to your child, success means not only coming up with new ideas, but from others acknowledging his vision.

If no one in your family shares your child's passion

for creation and invention, **try to find a like-minded mentor with whom he can brainstorm, or who can talk to him about how change doesn't always happen quickly or easily...particularly when it requires changing someone's mind.**

CHALLENGE 3 : FLAKING ON FRIENDS AND COMMITMENTS

While extraverted intuitives like your child love being around other people, they have a tendency to dive headlong into what seems most compelling—even if it means flaking on a long-standing commitment. Your challenge as a parent will be in helping him follow through. Two potential ways to do this are to:

1. put your child's top three goals on his whiteboard and make sure no new commitments interfere with these goals; and

2. plan friend "date" windows on certain calendar days and mark them in pen. If he is committed to a certain friend or activity on that day, don't allow him to switch or flake on commitments. After get-togethers, talk about how important support is in relationships and how proud you are of your child that he is a stable source of support for his close friends.

Handling Successes & Failures with an Extraverted Sensor

Nothing means more to your child than admiration from friends, teachers and family members. As such, one of the greatest gifts you can give your child is your acknowledgement of positive character traits and good choices.

This acknowledgement will also help temper your child's natural tendency to put a high value on superficial sensory things like fancy clothes, good looks, etc.

CHALLENGE 1 :: LIVING FOR THE MOMENT

While extraverted sensors like your child have a zest for life and do a better job of living in the moment than most other personality types, this present-focused mantra can lead to losing sight of longer-term goals. If the reason for doing homework, pursuing a passion or volunteering is so that it will someday look good on a college application or be helpful in the long run, your child is likely to forgo the activity for another that will benefit him most today.

For this reason, don't wait to celebrate long-term successes like grades at the end of the quarter. Instead, celebrate incremental and immediate achievements and make your praise very specific. For instance, "You made a thoughtful choice by helping your sister bring the groceries inside instead of finishing your video game."

CHALLENGE 2 : TAKING THINGS AT FACE VALUE

Because of your child's sensorial world view, he may tend to take things at face value rather than reading between the lines. Because of this, your child may end up misinterpreting relationships because he didn't fully understand what was going on beneath the surface.

If a relationship falters, help your child bring past events into focus, and how many straws building up over time can ultimately break the camel's back. Then, talk about what your child can do in the future to heal the relationship.

CHALLENGE 3 : FORGETFULNESS

Your child's tendency to forget about past commitments or assignments if he is involved in something interesting right now is one of the main challenges of the extraverted sensor personality type. Your challenge as a parent will be in helping your child remember what's coming up in the immediate term. Two potential ways to do this are to:

1. look at his daily calendar together and talk about what's ahead for the day, so that any commitments he made in the past are top-of-mind; and

2. talk about his nightly homework as soon as possible after he returns home from school. Decide when he will start his homework, then make sure he starts it at that time. Don't allow your child "just one more minute" or you may find yourself back at square one an hour later.

Handling Successes & Failures with an Extraverted Thinker

Nothing means more to an extraverted thinker than stability and assistance, or creating a structure by which he can more effectively standardize criteria for decision-making.

CHALLENGE 1 :: EQUALITY UNDER THE LAW

As an extraverted thinker, your child interprets the world through an organized set of systems and standards. Especially in times of struggle, his perception of unfair treatment by either a teacher or parent becomes magnified. As your child grows, enlist his help to establish rules and regulations for the family, as well as appropriate consequences. Strict definitions of success and failure make extraverted thinkers like your child feel most comfortable...and you may even find that your child relishes helping you enforce "family law." Similarly, in a classroom environment, just knowing the evaluation criteria for a class will help your child feel more confident that he is completing assignments "to the letter of the law," and will also give him talking points for a discussion with the teacher if a resulting grade is not what he expects.

Work with your child to create a reward structure, then celebrate achievements with expected rewards for the whole family. "You must be so proud of yourself!" or "I am so excited for you!" are irrelevant to your child. Rewarding both the sibling "team" and individual achievements in predetermined ways—especially if he was a part of creating the system—is both exciting and motivating for your child. Grading on a bell curve, subjective evaluations and sliding scales are in direct conflict with your child's need for impartial standards and rules. If a teacher utilizes these techniques, work together with your

child to create an objective criteria for success that you'll use at home to evaluate his efforts in class.

CHALLENGE 2 : WHEN THINGS DON'T GO AS PLANNED

Because of your child's desire for events to unfold in predictable, systematic ways, unforeseen obstacles or consequences can be challenging. When a project or task is assigned, help your child outline a project plan, and be sure to talk through some of the unplanned obstacles he may encounter along the way, and discuss how they will impact his overall timeline.

It's important to reinforce to your child on a regular basis that we sometimes need to re-think our original plans...both as kids and adults. Whenever things turn out in unanticipated ways, inspire your child by telling him that these new insights can lead to even more effective and streamlined planning in the future. Emphasize how timing needs to become more and more accurate, and how it's easier to side-step problems as we identify the specific hows and whys problems occurred. Then work on how to remedy problems quickly and get back on track. Acknowledge his identification of potential points of failure even if they DON'T occur and praise your child for living by the "5 Ps." (Prior Planning Prevents Poor Performance.)

CHALLENGE 3 : FEAR OF THE UNFAMILIAR

Because your child is so goal-oriented, he may stress out if he feels he doesn't have enough information to both determine the criteria for success and to develop an action plan. When this happens, work with your child to develop your own rubric together, along with the steps he does know he needs to complete on a project timeline. Then identify where the holes exist in his attack plan and take these documents in to the teacher to flesh out your child's map to mastery.

Handling Successes & Failures with an Introverted Feeler

Nothing means more to your child than close bonds with friends, teachers and family members. As such, one of the greatest gifts you can give your child is to place a high value on your emotional relationship with him.

A close, personal relationship will also help temper your child's natural tendency to avoid conflict because he will see you as a collaborator who "gets" him.

CHALLENGE 1 :: SENSITIVE SOULS

For introverted feelers like your child, emotion is the lens through which they prefer to interpret the world. Especially in times of struggle, whatever he is subjectively feeling will shade his perception of the challenging experience, subject or assignment. When he is struggling with a problem, don't immediately look for ways to fix the problem, just provide a shoulder to cry on. Don't try to rationalize his emotions, but instead remind him that you are there for him no matter what, and that you will get through this time together. It's not important to get to the factual specifics until after the emotional crisis has passed. At that point, ask if there is any way you can help, then you can start to work toward a solution together.

Be sure to celebrate both incremental and long-term achievements and make your praise feeling-, people- or relationship-oriented. For instance, "You must be so proud of yourself!" or "I am so excited for you!" Be ready to recall these positive outcomes in the event of test-based or assignment-based anxiety. For instance, "You got an A on your past essay with this teacher. I'm positive you can do it again!" or "When we talked to your teacher after you got the C on the last essay, she said the things

you need to focus on were A, B and C, which you've been doing. So you and I will be proud of your effort no matter what grade you end up with." Above all else, keep in mind that no feedback=negative feedback for sensitive souls like your child.

CHALLENGE 2 : ACCEPTING HIS FAULTS

Because of your child's emotional world view, he may tend to feel he has disappointed you or his teachers or coaches if things don't go as planned on a test or with an assignment. Your child may take a poor grade very personally and feel the mark is a reflection on him instead of solely his understanding or effort.

It's important to reinforce to your child on a regular basis that we are all human and imperfect. Whenever something comes up where another individual falls short of his goals, this is a great time to talk about how all that matters is whether the individual did his best and how failure isn't a permanent state, but just a way to show you the right and wrong paths to a successful outcome. Talking about other highly successful people's challenges and triumphs can be incredibly effective and inspirational for introverted feelers like your child.

CHALLENGE 3 : TACT VS. TRUTH

Your child's tendency to avoid conflict can lead to sweeping problems under the carpet or fudging the truth to avoid hurting someone's feelings. Show by example techniques that are both tactful AND truthful:

1. Show your child that he can be truthful and minimize hurt feelings by sharing intentions before critiquing his behavior or performance.

2. Be sure to clarify your expectations before you provide any feedback, and

3. reinforce after giving feedback that you are judging what he has done or how he has done it, not who he is, and that being able to trust each other to be truthful is a great way to have a closer relationship.

Handling Successes & Failures with an Introverted Intuitive

Nothing means more to your child than acknowledgement of his ideas and theories as valid and insightful. That's why one of the greatest gifts you can give your child is to play "What if?" with him.

Your acknowledgement will also help temper your child's natural tendency to buck authority because he will see you as a collaborator who "gets" him.

CHALLENGE 1 :: TO DREAM THE IMPOSSIBLE DREAM

For introverted intuitives like your child, future possibilities are the lens through which they prefer to view the world. It may even seem, at times, like he is not "with" you in the present, but dreaming up new solutions for a better world. Like Don Quixote, however, your child needs your encouragement to persist through failure after failure. Ultimately, your encouragement will solidify your child's self-perception and he will persist, thanks to the self-confidence he has developed.

For this reason, celebrate your child's "Why not?" attitude toward life. In the face of failure, remind your child of other dreamers—people who believed in themselves and changed the world, like Edison, Graham-Bell, Darwin, Columbus, and the Wright Brothers.

CHALLENGE 2 : COMMUNICATION BREAKDOWN

Because of your child's abstract world view, vague language and his tendency to make things more complex, he may have a hard time communicating not just with teachers but with peers and family members. Coupled with his preoccupation with inner thoughts and ideas and a fiercely independent nature, these characteristics can make effective communication or relationship maintenance a challenge.

Work with your child over the course of several conversations to note at least one or two situations, good or bad, that are happening with friends. If you notice a pattern, encourage your child to use his natural gift for reading between the lines to deepen the friendship. Remind your child that strengthening one-on-one relationships is equally as important as making the world a better place.

CHALLENGE 3 : THE ABSENT-MINDED PROFESSOR

Your child's tendency to live in theories and possibilities is the reason that he so often overlooks routine tasks, as introverted intuitives do.

Your challenge as a parent will be in helping your child stick to the systems you developed together in our chapter on Getting Organized and help him develop similar systems to employ during the school day so that important books, assignments or belongings aren't misplaced too often.

Handling Successes & Failures with an Introverted Sensor

Nothing means more to your child than admiration from friends, teachers and family members. As such, one of the greatest gifts you can give your child is your acknowledgement of positive character traits and good choices.

This acknowledgement will also help temper your child's natural tendency to put a high value on superficial sensory things like fancy clothes, good looks, etc.

CHALLENGE 1 :: THROWING THE BABY OUT WITH THE BATHWATER

For introverted sensors like your child, past experience is the lens through which they prefer to view the world. It may even seem, at times, like he is not "with" you in the present, but instead reliving a past experience.

Whatever outcome the past experience had may color his perception of the current subject or assignment.

For this reason, celebrate incremental and immediate achievements and make your praise very specific...and be ready to recall these positive outcomes in the event of test-based or assignment-based anxiety. For instance, "You got an A on your past essay with this teacher. Do you remember how she said your story structure was top notch?" or "When we talked to your teacher after you got the C on the last essay, she said the things you need to focus on were A, B and C. Let's figure out how to tackle those challenges in this assignment together based on what's worked for you in other classes in the past."

CHALLENGE 2 : TAKING THINGS AT FACE VALUE

Because of your child's sensorial world view, he may tend to take things at face value rather than reading between the lines. Because of this, your child may end up misinterpreting relationships because he didn't fully understand what was going on beneath the surface.

If a relationship falters, help your child bring past events into focus, and how many straws building up over time can ultimately break the camel's back. Then, talk about what your child can do in the future to heal the relationship.

CHALLENGE 3 : FEAR OF THE UNFAMILIAR

Your child's tendency to base decisions and conclusions on past experience is the reason that new and unfamiliar domains can be so uncomfortable for introverted sensors like your child.

Your challenge as a parent will be in helping your child contextualize new experiences or information. Two potential ways to do this are to:

1. remind your child of other things he has learned and steps that he has taken toward understanding, that followed similar patterns or processes; and

2. draw parallels to other environments or situations that either he or a historical figure has experienced, that have similar solutions or outcomes.

Handling Successes & Failures with an Introverted Thinker

Nothing means more to your child than stability and assistance creating a structure by which he can more effectively evaluate actions and reinforce decisions.

CHALLENGE 1 :: BROADENING THE CONTEXT

For introverted thinkers like your child, logic is the lens through which they prefer to interpret the world. Especially in times of struggle, his own objective evaluation will shade his perception of the challenging experience, subject or assignment. When he is struggling with a problem, he will appreciate you helping him look for ways to fix the problem. Get to the relevant factual specifics as quickly as possible so that he can find where the process flow fell apart.

Celebrate achievements with very specific, logic-

based praise. "You must be so proud of yourself!" or "I am so excited for you!" are irrelevant to your child. Instead, make comments like "now that you know X, you can start to understand Y" or "now that you know your teacher appreciated your insight on X, you can make sure you use that same technique to evaluate your Y assignment." Be ready to recall exactly what worked and what didn't work in the face of test-based or assignment-based anxiety. For instance, "When we talked to your teacher after you got the C on the last essay, she said the things you need to focus on were A, B and C. We've practiced those types of assessments during test prep, so you know how to include them when you problem solve on Friday's test."

CHALLENGE 2 : ACKNOWLEDGING OTHER PERSPECTIVES

Because of your child's logical world view, he may tend

to disregard or minimize other perspectives that don't fit into his understanding. It's extremely hard for him to compromise in order to reach consensus and peers or teachers may feel attacked by his devil's advocate positions. It's extremely important for your child to find order in chaos, particularly when under stress. Otherwise, he may resist changing his position because it doesn't make sense in his world view.

It's important to reinforce to your child on a regular basis that we sometimes need to re-evaluate our original conclusions based on new data and insights. Whenever things turn out in unanticipated ways, inspire your child by telling him that these new insights can lead to even more effective and streamlined decisions in the future and how thinking becomes more and more accurate as we identify specific hows and whys problems occurred. Acknowledge better decisions as they occur and,

if possible, which specific "learning lessons" from the past made the new decisions possible.

CHALLENGE 3 : TACT VERSUS TRUTH

Your child's tendency to fault-find can leave more feeling-oriented personality types feeling devalued when, in fact, your child shows respect to others through truth versus tact. Your challenge as a parent will be to help him transform problem *identification* into problem *solving*...in both school and relationships. A key part of problem identification in the relationship realm lies in effectively predicting, identifying and reacting to emotion.

1. Show your child that he can be tactful and minimize hurt feelings by predicting the other person's reaction and sharing intentions before critiquing their ideas or beliefs.

2. Reinforce that tact is an effective way of ensuring that others are open to his perspectives and more willing to listen to the careful analysis that brought him to his conclusions.

Teacher Communication

"Schools and parents are not really on opposite sides of any fence. But what does happen so often is that the school and the parent are running on parallel tracks, both hoping and striving in their separate worlds to give a child the best education."

~*Light Up Your Child's Mind.*

Renzulli, J. and Reis, S. (2009)

A *man once set forth on a journey with a horse and a donkey to carry his burden to his destination. Both animals carried their loads easily as they traveled along the flat plain. But when the group began to head up a steep mountain path, the horse found his load to be more than he could bear. He begged the donkey to relieve him of a small portion that he might carry the rest of the way, but the donkey refused. The horse soon fell down dead under his burden. Not knowing what else to do, the man piled the horse's load upon the donkey. The donkey, groaning beneath his heavy burden, repented, "If I had only been willing to assist the horse a little in his need, I should not now be bearing his full burden."*

The moral of this classic Aesop fable holds true of the relationship between parent, teacher and student. As your child continues his educational journey, both you and his teachers need to help him reach his graduation destination. You are making great strides by reading this book in order to help clarify and complete understandings for your child that may not have been achieved during the school day. However, you can also help to ease your child's teachers' loads by helping them understand the teaching approaches that will be most effective for your child, as well as help them get to know his likes and dislikes so that they have a good idea of the best ways to connect with your child—even before they meet for the first time.

You can use your child's Kidzmet® Student Snapshot as a way to "introduce" new teachers and tutors to your child, or you may just want to use the insights as a conversation starter and open lines of communication to let his new teacher know that you are willing and able to share the load by reinforcing at home what's being learned inside the classroom.

Ask what subject matter will be taught during the upcoming quarter and any techniques that will be used to teach the material so that you can augment the lessons without potentially confusing your child.

If your school is using the Common Core standards for language arts and math, you can download them here:

Language Arts:

http://corestandards.org/assets/CCSSI_ELA%20Standards.pdf

Math:

http://corestandards.org/assets/CCSSI_Math%20Standards.pdf

Another great reference that parents can use to support the core standards on the homefront can be found here: http://bit.ly/common-core-at-home

But don't let your involvement in school stop with periodic parent-teacher conferences or hallway conversations. One of the best ways to ensure a successful school year for your child is through a great relationship with his teacher. Remember that you, your child and his teacher are not adversaries, but together form your child's learning team.

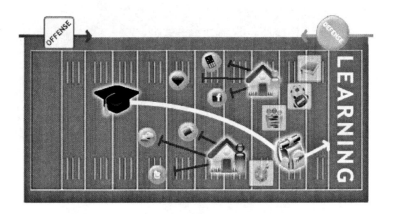

- The teacher's role on the team is to make sure that lessons connect with your child so that the lesson "pass" can be completed.

- Your child's role is to pay attention to the teacher, so that he can "catch" onto the lesson being taught...and practice regularly so that he can improve his game.

- Your role is to run interference on distractions that negatively impact practice time and let through extracurricular activities that spark your child's passion for learning.

Game On!

**Education is not the filling of a pail,
but the lighting of a fire.**
~William Butler Yeats

References

Armstrong, Thomas (1999). *7 (Seven) Kinds of Smart: Identifying and Developing Your Multiple Intelligences.* New York, NY: Penguin Group.

Armstrong, Thomas (2000). *In Their Own Way: Discovering and Encouraging Your Child's Multiple Intelligences.* New York, NY: Penguin Putnam.

Armstrong, Thomas (2003). *You're Smarter Than You Think: A Kid's Guide to Multiple Intelligences.* Minneapolis, MN: Free Spirit Publishing.

Bellanca, James A. (2009). *200+ Active Learning Strategies and Projects for Engaging Students' Multiple Intelligences.* Thousand Oaks, CA: Corwin Press.

Berens, Linda A. (1999). *Dynamics of Personality Type: Understanding and Applying Jung's Cognitive Processes.* Huntington Beach, CA: Telos Publications.

Birsh, Judith R. (1999). *Multisensory Teaching of Basic Language Skills.* Baltimore, MD: Paul H. Brookes Publishing Co.

Briggs Myers, Isabel, & Myers, Peter B. (1995). *Gifts Differing: Understanding Personality Type.* Mountain View, CA: CPP.

Briggs Myers, Isabel, McCaulley, Mary H., Quenk, Naomi L., & Hammer, Allen L. (1998). *MBTI Manual (A guide to the development and use of the Myers Briggs type indicator) (3rd ed #6111).* Palo Alto, CA: Consulting Psychologists Press.

Brualdi, Amy C. (1996). *Multiple Intelligences:*

Gardner's Theory. Washington, DC: ERIC Digests.

Buckingham, Marcus (2005). *The One Thing You Need to Know.* New York, NY: Free Press.

Christensen, C. (2008). *Disrupting Class.* New York, NY: McGraw-Hill.

Comer, James. (2004). *Leave No Child Behind.* New Haven, CT: Yale University Press.

Csikszentmihalyi, M. (1991). *Flow: The Psychology of Optimal Experience.* New York, NY: Harper and Row.

Csikszentmihalyi, M. (1997). *Finding Flow: The Psychology of Engagement with Everyday Life.* New York, NY: Harper and Row.

Cushman, Kathleen (2010). *Fires in the Mind.* San Francisco, CA: Jossey-Bass.

Dunning, D. (2008). *Introduction to Type and Learning.* Palo Alto, CA: Consulting Psychologists Press.

Fairhurst, A. Fairhurst, L. (1995). *Effective Teaching, Effective Learning: Making the Personality Connection in Your Classroom.* Boston, MA: Intercultural Press.

Fuller, Cheri (2004). *Talkers, Watchers, and Doers: Unlocking Your Child's Unique Learning Style (School Savvy Kids).* Colorado Springs, CO: Pinon Press.

Gansky, L. (2010). *The Mesh: Why the Future of Business is Sharing.* New York, NY: Penguin Group.

Gardner, Howard (1999). *Intelligence Reframed: Multiple Intelligences for the 21st Century.* New York, NY: Basic Books.

Gardner, Howard (2006). *Five Minds for the Future.* Boston, MA: Harvard Business School Publishing.

Gardner, Howard (2006). *Multiple Intelligences: New Horizons in Theory and Practice.* New York, NY: Basic Books.

Goleman, D. (1995). *Emotional Intelligence.* New York, NY: Bantam Books.

Haas, Leona, & Hunziker, Mark (2011). *Building Blocks of Personality Type: A Guide to Discovering the Hidden Secrets of the Personality Type Code.* Temecula, CA: TypeLabs.

Harris, Anne S. (1996). *Living with Paradox: An Introduction to Jungian Psychology.* Pacific Grove, CA: Brooks/Cole Publishing.

Hartzler, M., McAlpine, R., Haas, L. (2005). *Introduction to Type and the Eight Jungian Functions.* Mountain View, CA: CPP.

Hirsh, E., Hirsh, K., & Hirsh, S. (2003). *Introduction to Type and Teams.* Mountain View, CA: Consulting Psychologists Press.

Hirsh, S., & Kise, J.. (2006). *Work It Out: Using Personality Type to Improve Team Performance.* Mountain View, CA: Davies-Black Publishing.

Horstmeier, DeAnna, Ph.D. (2004). *Teaching Math to People with Down Syndrome.* Bethesda, MD: Woodbine House.

Hoyt, L. (2002). *Make It Real: Strategies for Success with Informational Texts.* Portsmouth, NH: Heinemann.

Jung, Carl G. (1976). *Psychological Types.* Princeton, NJ: Princeton University Press.

Keirsey, David, & Bates, Marilyn. (1984). *Please Understand Me: Character and Temperament Types.* Del Mar, CA: Gnosology Books Ltd.

Kemp, Anthony E. (1996). *The Musical Temperament: Psychology and Personality of Musicians.* New York, NY: Oxford University Press.

Kise, Jane (2007). *Differentiation through Personality Types.* Thousand Oaks, CA: Corwin Press.

Koch, Kathy (2007). *How am I Smart?: A Parent's Guide to Multiple Intelligences.* Chicago, IL: Moody Publishers.

Kroeger, Otto, & Thuesen, Janet M. (1998). *Type Talk: The 16 Personality Types That Determine How We Live, Love, and Work.* New York, NY: Dell Publishing.

Kuhl, P., Gopnik, A., Meltzoff, A. (1999). *The Scientist in the Crib: Minds, Brains, and How Children Learn.* New York, NY: William Morrow.

Lawrence, Gordon (1996). *People Types and Tiger Stripes: Using Psychological Type to Help Students Discover Their Unique Potential.* Gainesville, FL: Center for Applications of Psychological Type, Inc.

Lawrence, Gordon (1997). *Looking at Type and Learning Styles.* Gainesville, FL: Center for Applications of Psychological Type, Inc.

Lawrence, Gordon D. (2010). *Finding the Zone: A Whole New Way to Maximize Mental Potential.* Amherst, NY: Prometheus Books.

Maiers, A., Sandovold, A. (2011). *The Passion-Driven Classroom: A Framework for Teaching and Learning.* Larchmont, NY: Eye on Education.

McDonald, E., Hershman, D. (2010). *Classrooms that Spark!: Recharge and Revive Your Teaching.* San Francisco, CA: Jossey-Bass.

Meisgeier, C. H., & Murphy, E. (1987). *MMTIC Manual: A Guide to the Development and Use of the Murphy-Meisgeier Type Indicator for Children.* Palo Alto, CA: Consulting Psychologists Press.

Murphy, E. (2008). *The Chemistry of Personality.* Gainesville, FL: Center for Applications of Psychological Type, Inc.

Murphy, E. (1992). *The Developing Child: Using Jungian Type to Understand Children.* Palo Alto, CA: Davies-Black.

Oczkus, Lori D. (2003). *Reciprocal Teaching at Work: Strategies for Improving Reading Comprehension.* Newark, DE: International Reading Association.

Olson, Kirsten (2009). *Wounded by School.* New York, NY. Teachers College Press.

Payne, D. and VanSant, S. (2009). *Great Minds Don't Think Alike.* Gainesville, FL: Center for Application of Psychological Type.

Renzulli, J., Reis, S., Thompson, A. *Light Up Your Child's Mind.* New York, NY: Little, Brown and Company.

Schmidt, Laurel (2001). *Seven Times Smarter: 50 Activities, Games, and Projects to Develop the Seven Intelligences of Your Child.* New York, NY: Three Rivers Press.

Sharp, Daryl. (1998). *Jungian Psychology Unplugged: My Life as an Elephant.* Toronto, Canada: Inner City Books.

Silver, H., Strong, R., Perini, M. (2000). *So Each May Learn: Integrating Learning Styles and Multiple Intelligences.* Alexandria, VA: ASCD.

Sousa, David, et. Al. (2010). *Mind, Brain, and Education: Neuroscience Implications for the Classroom.* Bloomington, IN: Solution Tree Press.

Spoto, A. (1995). *Jung's Typology in Perspective.* Wilmette, IL: Chiron Publications.

Tieger, Paul D., & Barron, Barbara. (2007). *Do What You Are: Discover the Perfect Career for You Through the Secrets of Personality Type.* Canada: Little, Brown & Company Ltd.

Tieger, Paul D., & Barron-Tieger, Barbara. (1997). *Nurture by Nature: Understand Your Child's Personality Type - And Become a Better Parent.* Canada: Little, Brown & Company Ltd.

Tobias, Cynthia Ulrich (1994). *The Way They Learn.* Carol Stream, IL: Tyndale House Publishers, Inc.

Tokuhama-Espinosa, T. (2011). *Mind, Brain, and Education Science: A Comprehensive Guide to the New Brain-Based Teaching.* New York, NY: W.W. Norton & Company, Inc.

Walsh, Brian E. (2011). *VAK Self-Audit: Visual, Auditory, and Kinesthetic Communication And Learning Styles: Exploring Patterns of How You Interact And Learn.* Victoria, BC: Walsh Seminars Publishing House.

Willingham, Daniel. (2009). *Why Students Don't Like School.* San Francisco, CA: Jossey-Bass.

Willis, Mariaemma & Hodson, Victoria Kindle (1999). *Discover Your Child's Learning Style: Children Learn in Unique Ways - Here's the Key to Every Child's Learning Success.* New York, NY: Three Rivers Press.

Zichy, Shoya, & Bidou, Ann (2007). *Career Match: Connecting Who You Are with What You'll Love to Do.* New York, NY: AMACOM.

Numerous online reference sources including, but not limited to:

http://www.personalitytype.com
http://www.personalitypage.com
http://www.personalitypathways.com
http://www.businessballs.com
http://www.myersbriggs.org
http://www.personalitydesk.com
http://www.mypersonality.info
http://www.9types.com
http://www.discover-your-type.com
http://www.mbtitoday.org
http://www.psychologicalscience.org/journals/pspi/PSPI_9_3.pdf

Praise for Jen Lilienstein's Playbooks for Learning

"To say testers liked this would be a huge understatement."
The National Parenting Center

"When I read through [my son's] personalized book, I sat there with my mouth open – floored by the amount of detail and insight, revelation about my son. This is the kit every child should come with."
Lisa Fletcher for Parent Tested Parent Approved

"This workbook is easy to read, understand and apply. All parents should have one for EACH of their children."
Virginia Koenig, Learning Curve Radio

"I loved the interactive guidance and examples used. It will truly help all parents and teachers...allow to blossom the best that is truly in our children."
Roger Boswarva, Chairman, Ability Consultants

"With tips from preparing the environment to overcoming failures and even ideas for motivating your child, the Kidzmet Personal Playbook for Learning will be a valuable tool and a wise investment for assisting your child through their education."
Tabitha Philen, MeetPenny.com

"[What] separates this product from any other like it is the fact that through the use of the personality profile they are giving us {parents and teachers} the tools to successfully teach any child...A tool so valuable, it's worth it's weight in gold!"
Carlie Kercheval, SoYouCallYourselfAHomeschooler.com

"Armed with tools obtained from her Kidzmet Playbook,

we approached this...lesson a little bit differently... When the lesson was over, the teacher commented how amazing this turnaround was—a special one-of-a-kind 180...Thank you Kidzmet. You've armed us with knowledge that has truly changed our lives."
Kathy Gossen, CornerstoneConfessions.com

"Like is too small a word for how I feel about this book. Phenomenal is more like it. I want one for me!"
Felicia Danon North, Montessori Teacher

"The things I had already figured out about my children had come from over five years of teaching them, using trial and error. Yet every single thing I found out on my own was included in their Playbooks—and even more that I hadn't discovered yet!"
Jennifer A Janes, JenniferAJanes.com

"Overall, the book gives many helpful ideas as to what parents can do at home to help their child through school. It was an insightful read from which a parent could benefit. Teachers would benefit also. Even if they did not read the whole series, it would help them recognize the vast differences in how a child learns."
Kay McCafferty, KaysBookReviews.com

"Kidzmet, 'Kid Approved!'"
Amber Oliver, ClassicHousewife.com

"My initial impression of Kidzmet was, 'I don't need their help. I am a former school teacher. I know how to teach to multiple learning styles. I've got this all figured out. Anyhow, how could my four-year old even take the personality test.' I am eating my words...There were points that stood out to me. More like leaped out at me."
Jodi McKenna, GranolaMom4God.com

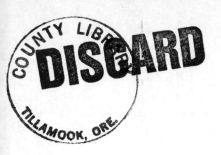